# FAILING HEART, UNFAILING HOPE

*My unforeseen journey from heart attack to healing*

FRAN DWELLE

WITH

JOE M. FERRANTE

**TO MY GIRLS**

Daughters:
Kaci, Jessica, and Cambria

and

Granddaughters:
Gianna, Flora, Harriet, Ruby, and Mira

*I love you.*
*You bring joy to my heart!*

# ENDORSEMENTS

"A moving drama of faith at the edge of death's abyss. A testimony to inextinguishable liveliness that comes when a person is gripped by the conviction that nothing is as real as God's love. Fran is my hero, a woman of great faith."

**Miroslav Volf**, Ph.D.
Henry B. Wright Professor of Theology at Yale Divinity School
Founder and Director, Yale Center for Faith and Culture
Author of numerous books, including *A Public Faith: how followers of Christ should serve the common good.*

"From the moment you open this book you will be gripped by this beautifully crafted narrative of a remarkable woman and her journey with a failing heart through to full health. Fran's unshakable faith will inspire you with the same hope that she put in her faithful God. Her compelling story allows you to share the warmth and cold of her experiences and to reflect on your own journey in a God who is always present."

**Carol Alexander**, Ph.D.
Dean of the Graduate School, Trinity Bible College
Author of *Simple Trust: Fifty Life-Changing Readings*

"Fran Dwelle has been a friend since our early days in Vienna together. I well remember the urgent prayer requests and ever-more dire progress reports on her behalf. But, as is recounted in *Failing Heart, Unfailing Hope*, the power of God's word and the prayers and faith of friends and family were abundantly evident throughout the painful ordeal. The reader will be blessed as this honest, powerful story unfolds, and your faith will be strengthened by this testimony of hope. It is my privilege to highly recommend this book."

**Dianne Collard**, D.Miss.
Montage International Director; ACT International, Europe Ministries Director
Author of *I Choose to Forgive* (expanded edition)

"In a world where our present and future circumstances seem so uncertain, Fran's gripping story speaks to us: there is one Presence—one strong tower—to which we can always flee to safety. Fran's life exhibits a unique synthesis of strong-willed determination and humble trust, and she shows us how to navigate the narrow path of walking in both wisdom and faith."

**Kate Bommarito**
Certified coach, Bomm Health and Wellness

*My flesh and my heart may fail,*
*but God is the strength of my heart*
*and my portion forever.*

**Psalm 73:26**

# Day One

The day my heart stopped, or didn't, dawned as Vienna's first beautiful spring day of the year. I could hardly wait to get out into the warm sunshine for my regular four-kilometer walk. I lived across the street from a section of the Vienna Woods, so I had easy access to several hiking trails. Depending on my mood for the day, I could walk through gently rolling hills, alongside beautiful vineyards, or on sloped streets in my neighborhood. My close Austrian friend Jeanette was my walking partner.

Since that morning's weather was so invigorating, we headed toward the steep *Himmelmutterweg* (Mother of Heaven Way) instead of taking our usual course through the woods. The pastel-colored houses along this walking route put on a grand display with their tile roofs and fieldstone chimneys, lace-draped windows framed by shutters and flower boxes, ornate fences and decorative gates, and manicured flower beds with sculpted hedges. Everything about these houses reminded me of the Austrians' love of beauty and pride of workmanship.

After returning home, I busied myself doing some household chores. My husband Arland was out, but my youngest daughter Cambria was home from school. I began cleaning the house room by room, eventually working myself to the bathroom. I scoured the tub for a few minutes and then suddenly stood up. Putting my hand to my head, I stumbled out into the hallway where my daughter was playing with her dolls. "Cami, I don't feel too well," I said. "In fact, I'm feeling rather dizzy."

At that very moment, Arland came in through the front door. He heard us talking in the hallway, so he came back just as I was trying to steady my balance. I said the same thing, "Honey, I'm not feeling too well. I started feeling dizzy when I was bending over cleaning the tub."

"Maybe you just stood up too fast," Arland said.

"No, something's not right. I'm feeling very strange. I'm dizzy and there's some kind of pain in my chest."

"You look very pale, Fran. Maybe you just need to lie down for a little bit." Arland took me into the bedroom and lowered me onto the bed.

I kept repeating, "Something's not right . . . it's just not right." Then suddenly I said, "Everything's getting black . . . I can hardly see." I felt myself slipping away and started moaning, "O Jesus . . . O Jesus."

Then I lost consciousness. In the next few minutes, Arland watched my skin turn dark, almost purple. My whole body became rigid, and I evacuated my bladder. My eyes were still open but Arland could see that I was fading. He tried again and again to find my pulse. He thought I was dying.

But after thirty seconds, I started breathing again with shallow gasps. I quickly drew a short breath, held it for a few seconds, and then let it out with a chattering sound: ch . . . ch . . . ch . . . ch . . . ch . . . This went on for two or three minutes. Again and again, Arland tried to find my pulse—checking my wrist and then the artery on the side of my neck, then back to the wrist, then back to the neck—but nothing. His mind raced as he tried to figure out what was wrong. Then he remembered I had complained of having chest pains.

"Mommy is having a heart attack," he said to Cami who was right there watching everything. "Quick, Cami, run upstairs to the Rapps! Tell them to call an ambulance! Mommy is having a heart attack!"

Cami was too scared to say a word. Clutching her doll, she bolted out the back door and raced up the stairs to the top floor.

She pounded on the landlord's door, and both Dr. and Mrs. Rapp quickly appeared. She blurted out in English, "My mom can't breathe! My mom can't breathe! My mom's blacked out! Daddy says she's having a heart attack!"

Mrs. Rapp was fluent in English and understood Cami. Right away they both ran down to our flat. Arland exclaimed that we needed an ambulance, so Dr. Rapp immediately called for one.

While waiting for the ambulance, my breathing became a little more relaxed and regular. But whenever I tried to speak, only gibberish came out. Arland tried talking to me, but I did not respond to anything he said. He feared I had suffered brain damage.

The ambulance quickly arrived with three paramedics. Arland was too shaken to communicate in German, so Mrs. Rapp translated for him as he told them what had happened. Without moving me off the bed, they quickly hooked me up to a portable electrocardiogram machine and began monitoring my heart.

After a couple minutes, the paramedic jumped up and shouted at Arland, "Where is her heart medicine? This is a very bad heart! This woman has a very bad heart! Why haven't precautions been taken? Where is her medicine?" Not waiting for an answer, he continued, "Does she have heart medicine? Does she have a history of heart troubles?"

"No, not at all!" Arland said. "She's never *ever* had any heart problems! Never!"

"Well, this EKG says she has a very bad heart," he said emphatically. He was irate with Arland and repeated the questions as if he thought Arland was not being truthful.

As they carried me out on a stretcher, I revived a bit. I looked at Arland and Cami as they lifted me into the ambulance, but I showed no signs of recognizing them. During the ambulance trip, I tried to speak a few times, but my choice of words made no sense, and the syntax was totally wrong. I would say, "No, no," because I knew the word was wrong, but I could not recall the appropriate word. I was completely disoriented, not recognizing anyone or anything.

When we arrived at the hospital, the paramedics rushed me to the emergency cardiac care unit. The doctors hooked me up on an intravenous drip. They also gave me an EKG, but this time it showed that my heart was normal. So, they repeated the EKG and got the same result—normal. This puzzled the doctors because they had assumed they were treating a heart attack patient.

So, they did more tests. A neurologist examined me by shining a light in my eyes and checking my reflexes in several places. Arland asked him, "Can you tell me what her problem is? Do you know what has happened to her?"

"I'm not sure what her problem is," he answered. "The only thing I'm able to say for certain right now is that it's not anything neurological."

The doctors ran a battery of more tests, but I was not aware of anything going on around me. After completing their tests, they moved me into the cardiac care unit where they could monitor my condition.

Four hours later, I began to regain consciousness. I was quite disoriented at first: *Where am I . . . How did I get here? . . . Who brought me here?* Then as the fog cleared, I thought to myself, *Where are my clothes? . . . Why am I lying in this strange bed without my clothes on? . . . And how were my clothes taken off of me? . . . And who had the audacity to undress me without my knowledge?* That last thought especially alarmed me.

Then a voice interrupted my thoughts. "Mrs. Dwell? Can you hear me, Mrs. Dwell?" With a slight German accent, he asked again, "Mrs. Dwell, how do you feel?" I turned toward the direction of the voice. Without my glasses on, everything was fuzzy, but I could make out the blurry image of a stethoscope hanging from his neck. Fully awake now, I heard a beeping monitor and smelled medicinal odors.

"Why am I here in this hospital?" I asked. "I'm feeling fine. Why are you asking me that? And why am I here?"

The doctor smiled, nodding in approval to my response. "Are you sure you feel okay, Mrs. Dwell?"

"My name is *DWEL-lee*, not *Dwell*," I said.

"I'm sorry, Mrs. DWEL-lee," he said, slowly emphasizing the correct pronunciation. "Are you absolutely certain you're feeling all right?"

4

"Well, yes. Yes, I think so. Why are you asking me that? Why am I in here? What's wrong with me?"

"Well, that's what we're trying to find out." He stopped talking while he poked around on my chest with the cold end of his stethoscope. After checking my pulse and blood pressure, he turned to leave saying, "I'll go tell your husband you're awake."

A few moments later Arland rushed into my room and greeted me with a big smile. He hurried over to my bedside, took my hand and asked, "Fran, how are you feeling?"

I could hear the anxiety in his voice. "Why are you asking me that? Did something happen to me? Why am I here in this hospital?"

"Honey, you blacked out at home, so I called an ambulance. They came and gave you an EKG and decided you were having a heart attack. So, they rushed you here to the hospital. You've been unconscious for several hours now while they've been running tests to find out what's wrong."

I was too stunned to reply. A torrent of objections flooded my mind: *My heart? My heart? How can that be possible? How could something be wrong with my heart? I've never been sick in my life; I exercise regularly; I watch what I eat; I don't drink; I've never smoked; I'm not overweight; I'm not diabetic; I don't have high blood pressure; I'm still young. What do you mean, "my heart"? HOW COULD SOMETHING BE WRONG WITH MY HEART?*

Composing my thoughts, I said, "I don't understand. This doesn't make any sense at all. I feel totally fine. Maybe I just overexerted myself this morning when I took a rigorous walk. Is that what they think happened? If not, then what *do* they think is the problem?"

Arland tried to reassure me. "Fran, don't worry. Whatever it was, the doctors now say you're out of danger. After looking at all the test data, they're pretty sure your heart is not the problem. But, on the other hand, they can't explain what went wrong. They're still puzzled about that."

I asked, "Are you saying that I was brought in here because I was having a heart attack, but now they're not sure if I ever had one in the first place?"

"Actually, now they're saying they're *certain* the problem has nothing to do with your heart. One of the doctors even told me a few hours ago that you're no longer in any danger."

"But you said the ambulance people took an EKG that showed I was having a heart attack?"

"Yes, I also asked the doctors about that, but all they said was that they can't explain the discrepancy between the ambulance EKG and the ER one. It seems to be a mystery to everybody here."

I said nothing for a few moments, trying to make sense of all Arland had said. Then I thought about my daughters, Cami, age 9, and Jessi, age 14. "How is Cami doing? Did she see everything that happened to me? And how is Jessi doing? Is anyone at home with them? They must both be worried sick about me."

"The girls are okay, Honey. Cami stayed with Dr. and Mrs. Rapp until Jessi got home from school. Then I went home for a while after they told me you were out of danger. Yes, the girls were very concerned, even afraid you were going to die. But I reassured them that you were doing better. I tried answering all their questions, and then I prayed with them before leaving. I also called the Mundises, and they agreed to look in on the girls." I felt relieved when I heard this. "Uncle Greg" and "Aunt Sandie" were close friends and missionary colleagues who loved and cared for our girls. We had met them nine years earlier when we began our Christian missions work in several countries in Eastern Europe.

Then I thought about our daughter who was at college in the States. "What about Kaci?" I asked. "Have you been able to get in touch with her?"

"Not yet, but I'll try again tonight. It's probably best that I didn't reach her earlier anyway, because now I can give her the good news that you're out of danger. There are many others who will also be relieved to hear you're okay. I had Cami call Pastor Danny right after we left for the hospital. Within an hour after your collapse, he had friends all over Vienna praying for you. And our missions headquarter also contacted people across the U.S. and Europe, asking them to pray for you."

Arland's report both encouraged and troubled me. "It's nice to know so many people were concerned for me, but why did everyone think my condition was so serious?"

"Well, Fran, it *did* look quite serious at first. Very serious." He paused for a few moments, trying himself to make sense of all that had happened. Then quickly he added, "But, thank God, the crisis has passed. Like the doctors say, you're no longer in danger. Try not to worry about anything and get some sleep. I'll be back in the morning." Arland prayed with me, kissed me goodnight, and left. Finding solace in his words and prayers, I soon drifted off to sleep.

Arland, however, had a long, sleepless night. Even though he had told everyone that I was no longer in danger, he was having trouble believing it himself. In his mind he replayed over and over the details of my ordeal that day. He kept asking himself, *How is it possible that Fran could have such a traumatic collapse one moment and then be declared "out of danger" a few hours later? How is it possible that the emergency team could shout that her heart was very bad, only to have the hospital say a few hours later that her heart was just fine? How is all this possible?*

That night I slept peacefully, grateful my ordeal was over.

But Arland wasn't so sure.

# Day Two

The next morning, I was released from cardiac care to a room in the general hospital ward. I felt perfectly normal, but the doctors wanted to keep me under observation while they ran more tests. Arland got Cami and Jessi off to school, and then he arrived at the hospital. He was elated to see how well I looked.

During the day, he accompanied me through test after test, asking each doctor and technician to explain what they were doing. They answered his questions and addressed his concerns as they ran their tests: EKG's, ultrasounds, blood tests, stress tests, treadmills, and neurological exams. Because the ambulance EKG showed I was having a heart attack, their tests all focused on my heart.

Arland had no trouble understanding everything the doctors were saying and doing. He had been intrigued by the field of medicine since he was a young man. He had even considered going to medical school before deciding on seminary studies. Although he was a pastor by calling, one of his favorite pastimes was reading medical journals. Arland's brother Terry, a physician and missionary doctor, also kept him current about the latest issues and developments in medicine. As a result, Arland had acquired a considerable amount of medical knowledge over the years.

As each test showed nothing wrong, Arland became increasingly troubled by their *we-don't-know* diagnoses. He pushed even harder for answers. He knew there had to be a reason for my collapse, so he would not rest until he got a satisfactory explanation. But no one seemed to have one. Adding more perplexity to the situation was the fact that I looked fine and felt normal.

Late that afternoon, Greg and Sandie came to visit. As they walked into my room, Sandie exclaimed, "Fran, you look as good as I've ever seen you! It's hard to believe that only twenty-four hours ago you were unconscious from a heart attack." In our years of friendship with the Mundises, we had walked through many joys and sorrows together. So, we had no doubt they would support us in this crisis. Both of them could hardly contain their joy as Arland shared with them the details of my recovery. Sandie's bubbly voice and Greg's booming laugh lifted our spirits, giving us a welcome respite from the intensity of that day.

A few hours later, while lying awake in the dark, I saw the door open slowly and someone peek cautiously around the corner. I instantly recognized the silhouette of Ginger Hall, the pastor's wife of The International Chapel of Vienna. She crept toward my bed, not sure whether I was awake or asleep. As she neared my bed, I spoke up, "Ginger, it's so good to see you."

"Oh Fran," she said with a start, "I'm so glad you're awake. From the reports we got, I wasn't sure if you were even conscious. How are you doing?"

"I'm feeling really great, Ginger."

"Well, thank God, Fran. We've all been so concerned for you since we heard about your collapse. I've already mobilized people in our church to pray for your recovery."

I was not surprised to hear this. Ginger was an energetic dynamo who accomplished whatever she set her mind to do. After four years of friendship, I had deep admiration for both her and her husband Danny. Ginger stayed only a few minutes, but her presence in the room gave me a big emotional boost. Long after Ginger and Greg and Sandie left, I found the positive effects of their visits still lingering with me. I ended my day by thanking God that my crisis was over and that I could resume a normal life in the morning.

# Day Three

The next day I was released from the hospital, less than forty-eight hours after I had collapsed. Every single test showed my heart to be perfectly normal. Since these findings contradicted the ambulance team's report, the doctors concluded that the ambulance EKG must have been in error. One of the doctors surmised, "Perhaps the EKG unit itself was faulty or unreliable because it was a portable machine."

Dr. Konrad Steinbach, the head of the hospital's cardiology unit and Professor of Medicine at the University of Vienna, came into my room as Arland and I were packing up my things. Surrounded by his medical entourage, he gave us his final report. "Well, Mrs. Dwelle, we do not know what is wrong with you or the reasons for all that happened to you. But one thing we can say for sure—your problem is not related to your heart. Your heart is perfectly well." And with that brief statement, he shook our hands, wished us well, and left.

As we were walking out the hospital building, Cami was skipping and singing for joy. Arland, too, was upbeat but he still had reservations. Several times he said, "Fran, I'm very relieved that you're feeling well again, but I wish, though, that just one person could tell us why you collapsed."

Arland could not let go of his insistence that there had to be a medical explanation for all that had happened to me. After only two days, it had already become his obsession. All the positive test results in the world could not convince him that my health was normal. "Remember, Fran," he reminded me, "I was the one there when you collapsed. None of those doctors were there. I know what I saw."

Without question, Arland had experienced my traumatic episode far more than even I had. *He* was the one who watched me lose consciousness. *He* was the one who saw my skin turn purple. *He* was the one who heard me stop breathing. *He* was the one who could not find a pulse. *He* was the one who saw death calling at my door. And deep inside, he knew—*he just knew*—everything was *not* all right. No matter what the doctors said! As far as he was concerned, when the hospital dismissed me, they dismissed too many questions—important questions, disturbing questions, life-and-death questions.

# Days Four to Thirteen

Arland began his search for answers the same day I came home from the hospital. He telephoned our family doctor in the States, who also was troubled that the Austrian doctors could not explain my collapse. Our doctor suggested that perhaps an aneurysm in the brain had caused it. He requested that I get to a major medical center in America as soon as possible and have a complete neurological and cardiac checkup. So, we began making arrangements to return to the U.S. in twenty-one days.

But five days after my release from the hospital, I began having mild chest pains. At first, they came intermittently. When I would lie down, however, the pains would completely stop. I had no idea what the problem was, but I felt assured—because of the recent hospital tests—that it had nothing to do with my heart.

When the chest pains persisted, however, both Arland and I became more alarmed. So, we intensified our preparations for leaving: purchasing airline tickets for departure in a week, informing the schools that our girls would be leaving, setting up medical appointments in the States, making housing arrangements in America, starting to pack.

Our mission board referred Arland to a renowned physician in Missouri; so every day he phoned that doctor to seek medical advice on my condition. Arland gave him all the details regarding my previous collapse and hospitalization. He asked the doctor why

I would experience chest pains while standing or sitting but not when lying down. He said, "I'm not sure why that is, but I'm pretty sure that it can't be her heart. Otherwise, the pain would persist whether she was standing, sitting, or lying down. Possibly, it could be something pertaining to her esophagus that acts like a 'fake' heart attack. Let's put her on a special diet of bland foods for a few days to see if that alleviates the pain."

So, for several days I ate nothing but oatmeal, yogurt, plain gelatin, and anything soft or mushy. However, the burning chest pain persisted under my left collarbone. Each day it came with more frequency and greater intensity. Yet every time I would lie down, the pain would go away within a few minutes. But as soon as I got up, it would return. My pulse rate dropped to sixty, and I was lightheaded, weak and listless most of the time.

Arland wanted me to go back to the hospital, but I resisted the idea. "Let's wait to see if it gets better," I would plead. "I think I can handle this pain a while longer, at least until we can get home to a hospital in the States." If I had to be hospitalized again, I wanted it to be in the States where the medical system was more familiar and my family was closer.

Troubled by my symptoms, Arland stepped up his efforts to find answers. He consulted daily with several doctors in the States, and they consulted with each other. When the bland diet didn't seem to help, they theorized that perhaps my collapse had caused undue stress on my brain and esophagus. But it was still conjecture. None of the American doctors had any definite answers either.

By Sunday morning, five days after the episodes began, the pain had worsened so much that I was starting to show visible signs of distress. Arland was monitoring my condition every hour, timing how long the pains lasted when I was up and how long they continued after I would lie down. By afternoon, the pain had become so bad that I could no longer bear it. Until then, I had hardly complained about it. But at that point I suddenly cried out, "Arland! I don't know how much longer I can handle this! It's getting so much worse! It's crushing my chest and going down into my arms!"

"That's it! We're not waiting any longer," Arland exclaimed. "I'm taking you to the hospital. We're going . . . *right now!*"

14

This time I didn't argue. Even though I wanted to hold out three more days for our flight to the U.S., I realized I could not make it that long. The pain had become too great. When I didn't respond right away, Arland repeated, "Now, Fran! We've got to go *right now!* If for no other reason, let's just go for *our* own peace of mind. If they tell us one more time, 'It's not your heart,' then at least we can rest assured that this pain is from something else."

Reluctantly, I agreed to go back to the hospital. In a few minutes, we were in the car. During the ten-minute drive, the chest pains became much worse. I was crying and moaning over and over, "Oh, Arland! It hurts so bad! It hurts so bad! Dear Lord, it hurts so bad!"

Arland was afraid that I was going to die before we made it to the hospital. Again and again, he despaired out loud (more to himself than to me), "I hope we haven't waited too long! I'm not sure we're going to make it! I don't care what they told us before— *this has got to be your heart!* Oh, Jesus, help us! Please! Help us!"

When we pulled up to the hospital, the *Wilhelminenspital,* a security bar blocked the entrance. Arland jumped out, ran up to the attendant in the booth and said, "My wife's having chest pains! She's having *severe* chest pains!" Immediately, the attendant lifted the bar and waved us through. Arland pulled up to the cardiology emergency entrance, the same place where the ambulance had brought me twelve days earlier.

I was too weak to walk to the entrance on my own, a distance of about 100 feet. So, leaning all my weight on Arland, I shuffled my feet in slow, small steps. When we finally made it to the emergency room, Arland told the registry woman behind the window, "My wife is having severe chest pains. I think she's having a heart attack."

She looked up at him, glanced over at me, and then asked casually, "How old is she?"

"She's forty-four."

She looked back at me and said nonchalantly, "Well, okay; take a seat. I really don't think your wife is having a heart attack, but we'll have someone check her in a few minutes."

I sat down. But Arland was frustrated with her apparent lack of concern. He went back up to the window and said, "My wife was admitted here less than two weeks ago with a bad heart, but she was released after nothing was found. I've got the test results right here from that earlier hospitalization."

The attendant took the packet of papers and said, "I'll give this report to the on-duty physician. Please have a seat and we'll call for your wife as soon as we can." So, we sat there waiting— waiting for thirty minutes—to be examined for a heart attack! Arland's frustration mounted the more it became obvious that no one there considered my condition to be urgent.

When the emergency doctor finally called for me, he did an EKG right away. Arland and I were dumbfounded—it showed that my heart was normal. Then he read through the medical report Arland had brought in. Since both the earlier hospital report and his own EKG showed nothing wrong, he said, "Mr. Dwelle, I'm not sure what your wife's problem is. She must simply be the type of person who has some kind of unexplainable medical crisis that *looks* like a heart attack but, in reality, it's something else."

Arland was not satisfied with that explanation. He shot back, "Then why the crushing chest pains? Why the pains down her right arm? Why the loss of strength and energy?"

"Well, I think it's probably just something that's stress-related." He turned to me and asked, "Have you been under a lot of pressure lately? Do you have a sensitive nature? Is there something going on in your life that's particularly stressful?"

"No, nothing at all," I said, "other than the stress I've had from dealing with this chest pain the last few days. Other than that, there's nothing unusual going on in my life."

He continued, "Well, I think you just have a very sensitive type of personality. There's probably some kind of *unconscious* stress that's causing your body to react physically. I don't think it's anything to worry about."

Arland asked, "Are you saying that there's nothing we can do then? That there are no more tests you can do? That we should just go back home?"

"Well, as long as you're here," the doctor said, "let's take a blood sample just to be sure it's not the heart. We'll have you wait out in the hall until we get the results back from the lab, and then you can go home." So, he drew some blood and sent it to the lab.

We found two chairs and sat along the wall in the dimly lit hallway of the emergency area. And again . . . we waited. I felt lethargic, even listless. Arland kept rubbing my back and asking every few minutes, "Do you have any more pain in your chest?" I still did have pain, but I saw no sense complaining about it since no one thought it was anything serious. Arland remarked that my color looked very bad, but I felt too groggy to carry on a conversation. I only wanted to go home. But we had to wait for the results of the blood work. So, for another half hour we sat on the hard, wooden chairs. Quietly waiting.

All of a sudden, the door at the far end of the hallway flew wide open, and two hospital attendants came bursting through. Pushing a gurney, they rushed toward the waiting area with the emergency doctor running behind them. Arland and I, along with everyone else in the emergency area, were startled by this sudden frenzy of activity. My immediate thought was, *Someone here has a real emergency! I wonder who this is for?*

To my total amazement, they stopped right in front of me. "It *is* your heart!" the ER doctor said to me. His whole mood had changed from the blasé attitude he had had thirty minutes earlier. He looked alarmed as he repeated to Arland in slow, deliberate English, "It *is* her heart, Mr. Dwelle. It's not getting enough oxygen!" The way he directed his words to Arland clearly conveyed, *You were right! Your concerns about your wife's heart were right!* He didn't say so in words, but Arland knew that he knew he had missed it. It was 6:30 p.m. Two hours—*two precious hours*—had passed in the emergency room before anyone finally made this diagnosis.

From that point on, everyone in the ER shifted out of neutral into high gear. Before I knew what was happening, two attendants lifted me onto the gurney and started racing down the hall. They whisked me into the elevator and hit the button for the cardiology floor. They wheeled me out a few seconds later. They rushed down the hallway and quickly pushed my bed into an empty ICU room. Immediately, several nurses swarmed around my bed and hooked me up to life-support machines.

The young doctor on duty recognized Arland from my previous hospitalization. He said, "Mr. Dwelle, you need to know that this is a major infarct. A *major* infarct! Your wife's blood test shows a highly elevated enzyme count. That means her heart has already experienced significant tissue death. She's had either a thrombosis or a blood clot that has destroyed the local circulation in her heart. Do you understand what that means?"

"Yes, I understand what you're saying. But what caused the blood clot to form? These things just don't happen by themselves, do they?"

"That's something we have no way of knowing at this time. All I can say for now, Mr. Dwelle," he paused as he shook his head back and forth, "your wife has had a very serious infarct. *Very* serious."

The doctor turned his attention to me and began assisting the nurse who was hooking up the heart monitor. He then helped the other nurses get me started on oxygen, intravenous blood stimulants, and blood thinners. They all worked together with a sobering sense of urgency . . . no wasted movements . . . no wasted words.

I watched all that was going on around me. My eyes saw it but none of it seemed real. I thought, *How could this be happening to me?* Yet in the midst of all the turbulence, I had incredible peace deep within my spirit. I thought, *God, I'm trusting in Your love and goodness. You will bring me through this. I don't know what it all means, but I know You will bring me through this.*

About 8:00 p.m., Sandie came to visit. Her smile quickly faded when she saw my condition. She stood close to my bed, holding my hand and speaking words of comfort. But she had trouble masking her shock. Every few minutes she muttered, "I just can't believe this, Fran. I just can't believe this is happening to my friend." Finally, she read a few Scriptures and prayed for me. Fighting back tears, she followed her *Amen* with a quick goodbye and left without saying another word.

A little later, I started feeling slightly better. The blood thinners and heart stimulants had begun taking effect, relieving most of the oppressive chest pains. But I was still reeling emotionally from the shock of this trauma. I kept telling myself, *I can't believe this has happened to me. After all, heart attacks only happen to other people.* But then I would be encouraged by thinking, *Since I'm already feeling better, it probably means that I'll fully recover in a week or so, just like many others have done after suffering mild heart attacks.* I even told Arland that I still hoped to lead the following week's JOY International breakfast, a women's ministry I had started six months earlier.

I did not know that my optimism was completely out of touch with reality. Ignorance, shock, and denial had worked together to impair my understanding of how critical my condition was. As I fell asleep that night, I was unprepared for the devastating consequences of this second heart attack.

Totally unprepared.

# Day Fourteen

B y the next morning, all my bodily systems had begun shutting down. The infarct had severely damaged my heart, drastically reducing its pumping capacity. In that weakened state, my heart could not provide adequate blood supply to my vital organs. The seriousness of this situation became increasingly obvious as the day progressed. I watched how Arland responded to the doctors each time they checked on me. I could see his despair— the more they told him, the more his spirits sank.

Sandie again came by that afternoon to see me for a few minutes. She stood close, holding and stroking my hand. She spoke softly, "Fran, we're all here for you. I know all of this is very hard to understand, but you're going to come through it." She tried her best to sound positive. But I knew her too well—I could hear the uncertainty and anxiety in her voice.

Many other friends came to the hospital that day to see me. Arland thanked them for their concern, but politely turned most of them away. A few were allowed in, including Bobby and Sheryl Beard, our missionary field directors. When they got the news about my heart attack, they cancelled their hectic travels in Eastern Europe and returned to Vienna. They stood with Arland at my bedside and prayed for my healing. Before leaving, they also prayed for our daughters, one by one.

The other visitor Arland allowed in was pastor Danny Hall from the International Chapel, one of the two Christian fellowships of

21

which we were a part. Accompanying Danny was Dr. David Melvin, another member of the church. Danny introduced him by saying, "Dr. Melvin is the director of the heart transplant program at the University of Cincinnati. He came with his family nine months ago to Vienna on a year's sabbatical to do research and development on mechanical hearts." Arland and I had seen him in church services, but we had never imagined he was a heart surgeon.

Arland gave Dr. Melvin a three-minute synopsis of all I had gone through during the previous two weeks. He finished by explaining, "Because the doctors told us ten days earlier that her heart was okay, we didn't think that these recent chest pains were in any way related to her heart."

"So, is that the reason you waited so long to come to the hospital this time?" Dr. Melvin asked.

"Yes, everything that was told to us by the doctors, both here in Vienna and also in America, led us to believe that it was not anything *that* serious."

Dr. Melvin was quiet for a few moments. Finally, he said, "Well, what *could* or *could not* have been done differently is all irrelevant now. The damage has already been done." He said it with kindness; he said it with compassion. He was trying hard *not* to add more pain to the anguish we already had. But like a cold winter gust strips off the last leaves clinging to a tree, his stark words blew away the last hopes Arland had for my recovery.

Dr. Melvin seemed to realize this, so he tried softening the blow by adding, "If I can be of help regarding any future medical decisions you may have to make, I'd be happy to make myself available." Arland quietly thanked him for the offer. He understood—far more than I did—the implications of what Dr. Melvin was saying.

By evening, the effects of the reduced pumping capacity of my heart became alarmingly apparent. Without sufficient blood supply, my organs no longer received the oxygen necessary to function properly. My kidneys could not eliminate fluids from my body, so my lungs began filling with water. As this edema worsened, I started experiencing serious breathing difficulty.

Arland shuttled back and forth between my room and the waiting area. He gave regular updates on my condition to the friends gathered out there. One of them told him that Kaci had been reached and would arrive the next day on a flight from the States.

About 10:00 p.m., Arland insisted they all go home until the next day. After everyone left, he collapsed into a chair beside my bed. For the second night in a row, he stayed close to my bedside in ICU, listening to me struggle for every breath.

He slept very little.

I slept even less.

# Day Fifteen

The next day saw my health deteriorate even more rapidly. By afternoon, I had become critical. In only forty-eight hours, the change in my condition had been catastrophic. About 5:00 p.m., the young doctor in charge took Arland into a conference room. "Mr. Dwelle," she began, "we've not had a chance yet to talk today. Tomorrow I leave for two weeks, and someone else will take charge of your wife's care. Before I leave, though, I need to tell you that your wife's condition has become very grave in the last twenty-four hours. Her breathing has become so bad that we're going to have to put her on a breathing-assist machine. It's a standard procedure for people with severe congestive heart failure. Her lungs are filling with too much fluid. Without this mechanical assistance she won't be able to breathe much longer. But you need to understand something else. Even with the help of this apparatus, her other organs probably will not be able to function much longer."

"Are you saying," Arland paused, "are you saying there's a chance that she could die tonight?"

She hesitated, searching for the right words. "Well . . . um . . . Mr. Dwelle, you need to understand something. *If* your wife survives tonight," she said slowly, "she will be an invalid the rest of her life. She will *always* have a very, very weak heart . . . that is, *if* she survives." She said it in a way that convinced Arland she had little—if any—hope for my survival. Arland reeled under the impact of her words. He already knew that my condition was bad, but he had not known it was *that* bad.

After the doctor left, Arland immediately went out into the hallway where friends had been coming and going all day. Greg was the only one there. "Greg, the doctor's just told me that Fran may not survive much longer. I'm going to have to tell the kids. We're going to have to say goodbye . . . just in case she doesn't live through the night."

Greg slumped over and buried his head in his hands. His body shook as he wept softly, crying between muffled sobs, "Oh, no! Please, God! Please, Jesus!" Arland and Greg wept together.

After a minute, Arland asked, "Can you help me, Greg? I don't think I can do this by myself. I need you to get my three girls and bring them here to the hospital. Kaci just got in this afternoon from the States. Jessi and Cami are already home from school. I don't want to leave the hospital because I'm not sure if Fran might slip away at any time."

Greg nodded, gave Arland a long embrace, and left to get the girls. Bobby and Sheryl came back to the hospital a few minutes later. Arland gave them the same news about my condition. He added, "Bobby, this is very hard to talk about right now, but I wondered if you would take care of the funeral arrangements in case Fran doesn't make it. I'm still hoping it will not come down to this, but we need to talk about it in case it does. I would like to have the funeral at Bethel Church in San Jose where Fran's parents are, and I would like Bob Schmidgall from Naperville, Illinois, to conduct the service." Bobby carefully noted the details.

While the three of them waited for Greg to return, Arland agonized out loud over the thought of talking to his daughters. "I dread having to tell my girls about their mother. How am I going to do this?" he asked them. "I just don't know how they'll take it."

About a half hour later, Greg and Sandie returned to the hospital with the girls. Arland left the Mundises and the Beards and took his daughters to another waiting area one floor down. The three girls huddled next to each other in a tiny, poorly lit alcove that no one was using. They sat silently, not knowing what to suspect and too afraid to ask. Finally, Arland forced out some words. "Well, girls, we're going to see Mommy in just a little while, but I wanted

to talk to you before we go up to her room. She's very, very weak."
He said the words slowly. "She doesn't even have enough energy to
talk, so we'll only be able to stay a short time. But I want to prepare
you for what you'll see, so you won't be too alarmed. They have
Mommy on a big machine made up of pumps and bellows. It's very
noisy, very distracting, and it covers her whole face. The doctors
are saying, you know, that she is very, very bad." He paused. His
voice cracked as he choked out the next words: "They think . . . they
think . . . Mommy might die tonight."

"No! No! No! No!" Kaci cried out, shaking her head back and forth.

Jessi closed her eyes tight, moving her lips in silent prayer.

Cami's eyes widened in terror, and she began crying softly.

Then all four of them cried together for several minutes. Finally,
over their muffled sobs, Arland led them in a brief prayer as they
held each other. When he finished, Kaci said, "I read a story recently
about someone who was supposed to die, but instead, she refused
to give up. That's what Mom needs to do right now. We need to
encourage her to keep fighting."

Arland asked them to dry their eyes and try smiling when they
entered my room. He did not have to spell out for them why they were
going up to see me. My three daughters understood clearly what was
happening—they were going to have to tell their mother goodbye.

Arland led them back upstairs. They walked through the landing
area where Bobby, Sheryl, Greg and Sandie were still waiting, and
then down the hallway to door #4 of ICU.

The girls walked into my room slowly, tentatively. They forced a
weak smile at me, but their expressions quickly turned somber as the
reality of my critical condition confronted them for the first time.
The whole intensive-care scene overwhelmed their delicate senses.
Pungent medicinal odors hung in the heavy air. A tiny fluorescent
tube cast deep shadows around the room. A dark curtain shrouded
my bed from full view. A huge black mask covered most of my face.
Tubes protruded from my mouth and nose. A breathing apparatus
hissed with my every breath. A beeping monitor broadcast each
beat of my weak heart.

They inched closer to my bed and Arland leaned over. "Honey,
we're all here. The girls want to say something to you. I'm going to
remove your mask for a few moments so that you can talk to them."

I was surprised to see the girls. I thought, *Why did Arland bring them in to see me in this condition? He should at least have waited until I was not hooked up to all these machines.*

But as soon as I saw their faces up close, I understood why. *They think I'm going to die,* I thought to myself. *That's why their eyes are puffy and red. That's why they look so traumatized. That's why they're all here. They think I'm going to die tonight!* No one had told *me* that I was on the verge of death. I did not know that an hour earlier the doctor had told Arland there was little hope. I *did* know that things were very serious, but I had never thought for one moment my life was in danger.

As Arland removed the breathing mask from my face, he said, "Fran, the doctors say that you are very, very weak. They say that your heart might not hold out much longer. We just want to tell you a few things." Turning to his daughters he said, "Girls, why don't you tell Mommy how you feel about her?"

There was silence for a few moments. Then Jessi spoke first. "Mom, I just want to tell you that I love you very, very much. I'm praying that you'll get better and that you will . . ." She broke down and began to sob.

Then Kaci spoke up. "Don't you give up, Mom. You fight! Fight! You fight, Mom!" Then she, too, started crying.

Cami did not even try to say anything. She climbed halfway onto the bed, almost lying on top of me, while she wept softly.

I waited a few moments, trying to compose myself, and then I responded. "Kaci my oldest, Jessi my middle girl, and Cami my baby, I know that the doctors say I'm very serious. I guess—" I stopped, gasping hard and struggling to catch my breath. "I guess they're saying that this could be my last night. But I just want you to know I'm believing God is going to bring me through this. But if He doesn't," I gasped for air again, "I want you to always remember that I love you . . . and . . . no matter what happens . . . don't ever, ever doubt that God is good."

Seeing how much I was struggling to breathe, Arland quickly put the mask back on my face. Then he said, "Fran, I also want to say something." He paused before continuing above the muffled cries of my girls. "Fran, you are the most wonderful person and the most special woman I've ever known. I'm so grateful that God gave you to me as my wife. I'm thankful that you are the mother of our three beautiful daughters. No girls could ever have a more loving and caring mother than you are. We are all so blessed to be able to love you and to be loved by you."

Arland and the girls then joined hands around the bed while he prayed, asking God for mercy, asking God to heal me. I felt like I was listening to my own eulogy. I could hear the words, but they did not seem real. I felt like asking, "Who are you talking about? Who is this elegant tribute for?" But while Arland was praying, I felt incredible peace in my spirit.

After Arland's prayer, each of the girls hugged me and kissed me and told me they loved me. Kaci again burst out in tears, crying, "Oh, Mom!" Turning around, they all stumbled out of the room together, barely able to stand up under the weight of their grief. Although they kissed me goodbye, they never actually verbalized it. That simple word *goodbye* was much too difficult to say.

As soon as they got outside my room, all three girls broke down completely, slumping onto the hallway floor. Their wails echoed down the corridors of the hospital floor. After a few minutes, they picked themselves up, ran out into the waiting area, and broke down again. Kaci collapsed into the arms of Aunt Sheryl. Jessi fell into Aunt Sandie's arms. Cami buried her head in Uncle Greg's chest. Each of them tried to comfort my girls, but their grief was inconsolable.

Meanwhile, back in my room—suddenly and distinctly—I heard the Spirit of the Lord whisper to my heart. *"You are not going to die,"* was the thought that came forcefully. At that moment, I recalled the Scripture verse from Psalm 118: 17—"I will not die, but live, and will proclaim what the Lord has done."

I had no doubt that the inaudible voice speaking to my spirit was the still, small voice of God. As He had done many times through the years, again that night God spoke to me through His Word. And *there*—in that hospital room, in the darkest moment of my life, when all hope was gone, when my body was all but dead— the Word of God came to me with *life*.

And I believed.

# Day Sixteen

For another hour that night, Greg, Sandie, Bobby, and Sheryl stayed with the girls at the hospital, holding them and comforting them. Most of the time was spent in silent waiting, waiting for another report from Arland, waiting to hear if I was still alive.

Finally, Arland asked Greg and Sandie to take the girls home. But first, he took Greg aside. He began, "Greg, I'm not going to leave Fran tonight . . . so if . . . um . . . if she dies . . . sometime . . . um . . . sometime during the night . . . well . . . I'll phone you right away . . . but . . . um . . . Greg . . . this . . . this is really hard . . . hard for me to ask . . . but . . . would you . . . I mean . . . do you think you would be willing . . . to tell the girls about . . . you know . . . about Fran's death . . . if that happens?" Greg's eyes welled up with tears. His lower lip quivered as he nodded his assent. Before turning to leave, Greg and Arland shared a silent embrace,

On the way home in the car, no one said a word. Cami looked out the back window at the dark sky and prayed quietly, "God, why did this happen? My mom's going to die tonight, and then what's going to happen to me? I'm only nine years old. How can I take care of myself? And who's going to raise me? Is Kaci going to come back home and take care of me? How will I be able to grow up without a mom?"

When they got to our house, Greg and Sandie sat with them on the couch, holding them., talking with them about their fears, and listening to their questions. Sandie consoled them by saying, "Girls, God loves your mom even more than we do. And He also knows how much you need her. I know it's hard, but we have to trust God with things that are out of our control. Even if your mom dies tonight, God will never abandon you. He'll always be right there to love you and comfort you." Her calming words soothed them enough so they could finally go to bed. Then Sandie went home, but Greg stayed, bedding down on the living room couch.

As the Beards drove home from the hospital that night, the stress of dealing with my 48-hour crisis took its toll on Sheryl. She experienced a sudden episode of intense pressure and chest pain. She was unable to breathe; she felt clammy; she had heart palpitations; she became panicky. So, Bobby immediately took her back to the hospital emergency room. After several hours of testing, the doctors concluded that her body was reacting to the trauma that her friend (me!) was going through. They prescribed sedatives and put her on complete rest for a week.

At my home the next morning, Greg, Kaci, and Jessi were up early, quietly talking around the table. Then the phone rang. All conversation stopped as Greg picked up the phone. He listened silently, saying only, "Yes, Arland . . . yes . . . okay . . . yes, Arland, I'll tell them." And with that he hung up.

Awakened by the phone, Cami walked out into the dining area a minute later. When she saw everyone whispering together around the table, she asked, "Was that Dad who just called? Is Mom still alive?"

"Yes, that was Dad," said Kaci.

"And yes, Cami, Mom *is* still alive! She made it through the night."

# Day Twenty

'D o you know what day this is, Arland?" I had been awake in my hospital room for an hour, waiting for him to wake up. Arland uncoiled from the reclining chair he had slept in for eight straight nights.

"Well yes, Fran, actually I do know what day it is. Today is Sunday, Palm Sunday."

"Well, I guess we'll have to hold our own church service today. Right here in my room. Why don't you read something from the Bible, and then we can pray together. Maybe the Lord has something more from the words in Psalms 20 through 30 that will encourage us today. Would you read to me again from those psalms?"

In the seven days since my hospitalization began, I had received dozens of cards, letters and faxes from people around the world. Many had included Scripture verses of encouragement. Arland and I had marveled at how many of the references were from verses found in Psalms 20 to 30. So, after reading one of those psalms each day, we would focus our prayers on some aspect of God's character described in that day's reading.

Arland began reading **Psalm 20:**

### "May the Lord answer you in the day of trouble!" (NKJV)

Those words were such an appropriate description of the last seven days of my life. Each one had been a "day of trouble" unlike anything I had ever experienced before. And each time I faced a new crisis, the Lord *did* answer my heart cry for help! In the hours after Arland and my daughters said goodbye, my lungs filled up with fluid, and my breathing was no longer spontaneous, but with each wave of panic came a prayer to my lips: "Oh, Jesus, please help me, please help me breathe." And the breathing-assist machine would keep me going. Arland also prayed every time he woke up that night. First, he would glance at the heart monitor to see if I was still alive. Then, after seeing my heartbeat at only 60, he would pray, "Please, Lord, get her heartbeat up to 90." And the Lord *did* answer his heart cry for help.

Arland moved on, reading from **Psalm 21:**

**"Be exalted, O Lord, in your strength; we will sing and praise your might."**

God had certainly shown me His strength and power when I thought I was going to suffocate those first few days. The doctor had warned me that few people could stand the oppressive weight and force of the passive breathing apparatus that covered my entire face. But I had determined, with the Lord's help, that I would do it. And He did give me strength to endure it. After four days, my breathing had improved—only a little—but it was enough to get that dreaded black mask removed from my face.

**"My strength is dried up . . . and my tongue sticks to the roof of my mouth."**

Arland read from **Psalm 22.** For five days I had experienced a raging thirst unlike any physical craving I had ever known. My kidneys had stopped working, so my lungs would fill up with water. The doctors put me on diuretics to help eliminate water from my body, but they only intensified my thirst for water. My total intake of water was limited to just one liter a day, an amount that seemed like *no water at all* when compared to the voracious thirst I had. Sheryl brought me a fruit slush each day to alleviate my raging thirst, but *nothing* could take away my obsession for a drink of water. More than once I sighed, "What I would give for a huge cold glass of Diet Coke!" When I felt like I was going to die of thirst, the Lord helped me endure this.

34

**Psalm 23**—I had memorized this famous psalm as a child. Now it really came to life.

**"Even though I walk through the valley of the shadow of death, I will fear no evil, for you are with me."**

In my dark and difficult days, I found a source of strength, courage, and confidence in Christ. He was with me! Any fear gave way to a quiet trust in His love and presence.

**Psalm 24** said,

**"Who is this King of glory? The Lord, strong and mighty."**

Without a doubt, the Lord's strong character was my anchor in this storm. Each day I meditated in my hospital room on the names and attributes of God in Scripture. These eleven psalms were filled with different names of God: my Shepherd, my King, Most High God, Strength of My Life, my Salvation, my Light, my Rock, my Shield, my Refuge and my Helper. By focusing on God's character, I found an inner peace in the midst of uncontrollable chaos all around.

**"The troubles of my heart have multiplied; free me from my anguish."**

Arland read from **Psalm 25**. How appropriately this Scripture described my situation. Heart troubles! I would have never thought I would have major heart troubles. But the bigger issue was *why*. Why do I have heart problems? And why can no one answer that question? Again and again, Arland had asked the doctors, "What has caused this to happen to my wife's heart?"

Their answer was always the same: "We're not sure at this time." Then they would hypothesize, "Maybe she had a defective heart for years, and it's only been detected now. Or perhaps, there was a narrowing of her coronary arteries that restricted the blood flow to her heart." But in my critical condition, I was too weak to undergo an angiogram to see if there was a blockage in my arteries.

**"I have trusted in the Lord without wavering . . . For your love is ever before me."**

These words from **Psalm 26** caused me to marvel at how God's love had sustained me through seven days of one heart exam after another. Two days earlier, Dr. Guenther Laufer, director of the heart transplant program at the General Hospital of Vienna (commonly called "The *AKH*" for its German name, *Allgemeines Krankenhaus)*, had given me the results of the heart exams. "Mrs. Dwelle, the crisis you have experienced has left permanent damage to your heart. Over three-fourths of your heart muscle has been destroyed, and you cannot function for long with a heart that has only twenty-five percent of its pumping capacity."

I anticipated where he was going with this discussion. *He's trying to break the news gently that I need heart surgery,* I thought. *Probably a bypass or something like that.* But his next words caught me by surprise: "You need a heart transplant as soon as possible. It's your only hope. But we can't do one right now because you're not strong enough. We'll have to hope you'll improve some before we can put in a bid for a heart."

I was stunned. The thought of a heart transplant had never entered my mind. I could not comprehend that my condition could ever be that grave. Yet, despite the negative report, I resolved to never waver in my confidence in God's goodness. Nothing—not even this crisis—could separate me from God's love.

Arland continued onto **Psalm 27:**

**"I am still confident of this: I will see the goodness of the Lord in the land of the living. Wait for the Lord; be strong and take heart."**

This affirmation of God's goodness caused my spirit to well up with praise. I can honestly say that I had never doubted God's goodness for even one day in my life. During our years pastoring in Wisconsin and doing Christian ministry in Yugoslavia, God's goodness had been the one unshakeable constant in every crisis I experienced. Although this latest trauma was far more critical than the others, I would not succumb to despair.

From **Psalm 28,** Arland next read the verse that had become one of my favorites:

## "The Lord is my strength and my shield. My heart trusts in Him and I am helped."

If ever I needed God's strength, it was now. When I saw my body struggling to perform even the simplest functions—breathing and sleeping—I realized how much I needed God's power and energy to face what each day brings. Often, I would find myself silently quoting the words, *The Lord is my strength . . . and I am helped . . . yes, I am helped . . . I am helped.*
**Psalm 28** adds,

## "My heart leaps for joy, and I will give thanks to Him in song."

In my critical condition, I wondered if I could give thanks. Then I realized there still were many things for which to be thankful. So, I thanked God for who He is and what He can do. I thanked Him for Arland, our three daughters, friends, and family members who loved, encouraged, and prayed for me, for the caring Austrian doctors and nurses working their best to keep me alive, and for the many scriptural promises which strengthened and encouraged me.

Arland read the descriptive title for **Psalm 29:**

## "The Voice of the Lord in the Storm"

How appropriate *the storm* was as a metaphor for my experience! After my first collapse, I felt relieved that the storm clouds from that crisis had quickly dissipated after a brief cloudburst. Arland, however, suspected all along that those first clouds forewarned of a far more serious storm waiting to move in. Unfortunately, *his* forecast had been the correct one. That first collapse had been merely the front edge of a massive storm system that unleashed all its fury two weeks later with my second heart failure. After that storm had passed, all my hopes for a healthy life lay submerged beneath its floodwaters. But this psalm reminded me that the Lord **sits as King of the flood.**

**Psalm 30** was entitled **Thanksgiving for Deliverance from Death.** The Psalm says,

## "I called to you for help and you healed me."

So, that night Arland and I asked God for that very thing—a healing. We prayed, "Lord, Your Word tells us you are present in the midst of the storm. So then, would You please come, Lord, into this storm of our lives and give us a visitation of Your presence and Your power?"

When we asked that night for a *visitation*, we did not mean, of course, a *literal* visitation from God. Rather, in our prayer terminology, *visitation* was a figurative term we often used to signify God's healing presence. My body needed a miraculous healing, *i.e.*, a visitation from God, or else I was going to die. *That* was the type of *visit* we requested from the Lord that night. Never once did we think that asking for a visitation from God meant asking Him to visit us *in person*. Never once in our prayers on that Palm Sunday evening. Never once in our prayers at any time in the past.

Never . . . ever . . . once.

# Day Twenty-One (1)

That night, in the early morning hours, I awoke with a start. Immediately, I glanced at the clock on the wall. After eight unbearably long days and nights in ICU, both Arland and I had become obsessed with time, right down to the minute. It was 3:05 a.m. I was sure of it.

My eyes scanned the room. The door in the far-right corner was closed. Arland was asleep in the chair along the left wall. No one else was in the room.

All of a sudden, a ball of bright light appeared in the far-right corner, in front of the closed door. I raised my head slightly to get a better look. In a few seconds, the light enlarged.

Suddenly, Jesus appeared. He entered my room through the closed door.

He stood still for a moment in front of the door, emblazoned in His glory. A glistening robe flowed down to His feet. A soft bluish-white luminescence outlined His body. An ethereal glow veiled His face.

My heart pounded as I watched.

He walked slowly across the room.

He stopped at the foot of my bed. He stood before me in majestic silence. He stretched out His hands over me. He covered me with a blanket of light. Immediately, I felt power emanating from His hands to my body

I felt warmth flowing through me from head to toe.

I felt compassion bonding my spirit with His.

I transfixed my eyes on Him, never turning my gaze away, not even for one moment.

I felt absolute awe in His presence. I had no fear. None. Just total delight.

I had no consciousness of self, only of my Savior. I lost awareness of everything temporal. I was in the presence of Eternity.

Time stood still.

And I worshiped Him. Suddenly, I realized that the Lord was standing in a place where He eclipsed the crucifix on the opposite wall. I thought, *Yes! That's how it should be! You are the resurrected Christ! You have conquered death to bring life! For days now, I've been suspended between life and death. But You are the bridge between the two!* And I worshiped Him.

Our communion together lasted a few seconds or a few minutes or . . . much more. In his presence I had no sense of time.

Finally, Jesus turned around and slowly walked away. He left the same way He came in—*through* the closed door in the corner of my room. Just like that, He was gone. Instantly, I felt strength in my physical body. I *knew* the Lord had come to heal me. I was absolutely certain of it because I felt completely renewed. Immediately, I cried out, "Arland! Arland! Wake up! The Savior was here! Did you see Him?" Arland was instantly awake. Alarmed, he shot up from his chair, glancing at the clock on the wall.

"Arland, did you see him? The Savior was here! I'm healed! The Savior was just here! Did you see Him, Arland?"

He rushed to my bedside. Leaning over, he asked, "What are you talking about, Fran? Are you all right? What's happened?"

"Arland, the Savior was here! He visited me! He came to heal me! Did you see Him?"

Arland hesitated to say anything, not sure if I was fully present or if I was experiencing my final moments before dying. I exclaimed again, "Arland, I'm healed! I know I'm healed! I can't wait for the doctors to take their tests. They'll see the changes. I know they will. Because I'm healed! The Savior came and healed me! Did you see Him?"

In a soft tone, Arland said slowly, "No, Fran . . . No, I didn't see anything. I guess I must have been sleeping. What happened? Were you asleep? Are you saying that you had a dream? Or was it some kind of a vision you saw?"

"No, Arland, I was *not* asleep. I was *not* seeing a vision. The Savior was here! Right here in this room! He was here . . . *in person!*"

As I related the entire incident, Arland listened at first with more than a little doubt. But seeing how animated I was, he soon realized something quite unusual had transpired. He cautiously remarked, "I'm not sure what has happened to you. But I can see that your breathing is much better, and your pulse rate is up. So, I guess we'll have to wait and see what the doctors say in the morning."

As we talked more, I marveled that God had answered our petition for a healing *visit* in such a literal way. I had *absolutely no doubt* that the Lord had come in person for one reason and one reason alone—to heal my damaged heart. And I felt so alive! For me, that was proof enough that He had already begun that healing.

We decided not to tell anyone about the Lord's visit until the doctors confirmed that I was totally well. Until that happened, we agreed to keep this experience hidden in our hearts.

After I drifted off to sleep, Arland stayed awake another hour, trying to comprehend all that had just transpired. Before falling back asleep, he opened up his small personal diary. Always meticulous in his record-keeping, he made the following brief entry in his little black book:

*M o n d a y, A p r i l 1 3, 1 9 9 2*
*Fran woke me up at 3:10 this morning saying,*
*"Arland! Arland! The Savior was here!*
*Did you see Him? Did you see Him?"*

For me, this encounter had transcended all sense of time. But actually, the Visit had lasted five minutes. Five minutes of holy Presence. Five minutes of loving Presence. Five minutes of comforting Presence. Five minutes of healing Presence.

One thing I knew for sure: my life would never be the same.

Jesus had visited me and my heart was healed!

# Day Twenty-One (2)

When I woke up a few hours later, Arland was already awake. Without even a *good morning*, his first words were, "Look, Fran! Your urine bag is full!" He was so excited about it that I had to laugh. But I understood his elation—a full urine bag meant my kidneys were functioning again. And that meant my heart was pumping more blood. And that meant something must have changed drastically during the night!

When the nurse came in to check my vital signs, she was surprised at how much I had improved. Then the doctors ran their normal regimen of daily tests: heart exams, lung and kidney exams, and blood samples. Every doctor commented that I looked so much better than I had before.

Arland and I waited with great anticipation for the test results. Late that afternoon, the head physician came into my room accompanied by his entourage of doctors and nurses, about 10 people. "We don't understand everything, Mrs. Dwelle, but we're delighted that your condition has improved significantly. All your vital signs are improved. Your kidneys are functioning, and your lungs are draining of fluid. In fact, you've improved enough that we're going to take you off the critical list." He took out his charts and showed us the positive changes in my vital signs.

"I'm glad that all those things are better," I said. "But doctor, you haven't said anything about my heart. *What about my heart?* Is my heart better?"

The doctor glanced at Arland before directing his words to me: "Mrs. Dwelle, your heart shows little, if any, improvement."

"Does this mean that you think a transplant might still be necessary?" I asked.

"Well, all we can say for sure is that a transplant is not as *urgent* a consideration today as it was yesterday."

"Well, good! Because a transplant is totally out of the question," I said. "I would never agree to something that drastic."

He paused before responding. "Mrs. Dwelle, please don't misunderstand what's happened here. You *are* doing much better today, but you're *not* out of danger yet. Your heart has barely improved at all." Turning to leave, he added, "We're happy about all these other improvements, but to tell the truth, your heart is still very bad."

His parting words left me totally confused. I pondered them throughout the evening. *Why Jesus?* I prayed silently. *Why am I not healed? You came to my room. I felt your presence. I felt your power. I've been praying for healing and I am better. But Lord, I'm still not healed. I don't understand why You appeared to me if it wasn't to totally heal my heart. Even though none of this makes sense, Lord, I want to tell You that I still trust in your love and in your perfect timing. And I'm still totally confident of one thing—You will complete the healing you've begun today.*

In spite of the perplexing report, my spirits remained high. I knew my *why* questions would soon be answered when Jesus completed the healing He had begun. *After all,* I told myself, *why not? Why wouldn't God complete what He had already started?*

# Days Twenty-Two & Twenty-Three

When I awoke the next day, I felt even stronger. In the afternoon, my father came to visit with Cami. My parents had arrived in Vienna four days earlier from California, but the day after their arrival my mother broke her kneecap in a fall. Disappointed that Mom could not visit me, I inquired about her health. After reassuring me that Mom was on the mend, Dad asked, "Honey, can I read anything to you from the Scriptures?"

I knew my father loved the Bible because he had read it daily for more than 50 years. As a young girl, I would listen to him read the Bible in the evenings for our family devotions. His resonating voice seemed to make the words come alive. "Yes, Dad," I said, "would you read to me from Psalm 30? It's become one of my favorites since I've been in here." As he was reading, the words from verse 3 again struck me: "O Lord, you brought me up from the grave, you spared me from going down into the pit."

Just as Dad finished reading, I began getting tingles all over my body. I tried to speak but nothing came out. My father noticed that my lip was drooping on one side, so he quickly called for help. When the nurse came, she took one look at me and called for the doctor. He arrived a few moments later, quickly examined me, and said, "Mrs. Dwelle, we're going to run some tests right away to see what's happened."

Arland walked into the room just as they were wheeling me out into the hall. Right away he noticed the muscle distortion on my face. "What's wrong?" he asked.

"Your wife's just had a stroke," the doctor said. "We don't think it's a major one, so we're hoping the symptoms will disappear. But we need to give her a CAT scan to see if there's any intracranial bleeding."

When the results of the CAT scan came back, everything was negative. There was no evidence of any bleeding in the brain. In fact, by evening most of the symptoms had disappeared, and I had regained almost 100% of my speech. Because I recovered in less than 24 hours, the doctor termed the incident a *transient ischemic attack* instead of a stroke *(ischemia* referring to a stoppage or clogging of the blood in an artery or the brain).

Even though this incident was milder than the previous two, it raised even bigger questions in Arland's mind—questions he had never thought of before. *Is this latest transient ischemic attack related to the earlier so-called heart attacks? And if so, how? And what is causing these incidents? Is it just because Fran has a bad heart? Or is it possible that her heart is not the cause of these problems? What if something else is causing these incidents? Something like a blood clot? And if that's the case, then what is causing these blood clots to form? And where do they come from?* Throughout the night and into the early morning hours, he grappled with these questions, searching for an explanation that made sense.

The next morning, when the doctor came to check me, Arland stopped him at the door as he was leaving. "May I ask you something about Fran's condition?"

"Yes, Mr. Dwelle, what is it?"

"Well, I've been thinking," Arland began, "this is the third ischemic incident my wife has had. We know that yesterday's one was in her brain. The second one, the one that caused all the damage, was in her heart—no doubt about that. And the first one . . . well . . . the first one came and went without anyone being able to explain whether the problem was in her heart or her brain or anywhere else for that matter. All along, though, we've been assuming that she either has a defective heart or else some degree of narrowing in her coronary arteries. But is it possible that neither of these conditions caused Fran's heart problems?"

"What makes you question that?" he asked.

"Well, I've been wondering, is it possible that the problem never was with her heart to begin with? Could it be that the problem is related instead to something going on with her blood?"

"What do you mean?" he asked.

"Is it possible that she has some kind of condition that causes clots to form in her blood? And if that's the case, could her first collapse have been caused, not by a bad heart or bad arteries, but by a blood clot that went to her heart?" When he did not respond, Arland asked, "Are you familiar, Doctor, with the details of that first incident over three weeks ago?"

"Go on, Mr. Dwelle, refresh my memory."

"Well, the ambulance attendants who came to our home took their EKG and concluded that Fran was having a heart attack. They were absolutely certain about it. But the next day, the doctors here at the hospital said that their EKGs showed that she had never had a heart attack in the first place. I asked them for an explanation, but no one in the hospital could account for the discrepancy between the two EKGs.

"But I've been thinking . . . and this is what I want to ask you . . . is it possible that a blood clot caused the first heart trauma . . . and the ambulance EKG just happened to record it at the moment it was occurring . . . but the clot then passed on through without permanently damaging her heart . . . which would explain why the hospital EKG taken an hour later showed nothing abnormal with her heart? Can you tell me, Doctor, is this scenario even a remote possibility?"

The doctor was silent for a few moments. Then he said, "Well . . . yes, Mr. Dwelle, you may have something there."

"So, if that could explain what happened the first time," Arland continued, "then wouldn't it be possible that the second incident . . . the one which left her heart so severely damaged . . . could also have been caused by a blood clot . . . but because this second clot was much bigger than the first one . . . it didn't dissolve or pass on through her heart like the first one did . . . but instead it blocked her circulation long enough to destroy most of her heart?"

Arland paused for a response, but the doctor just kept his eyes bored on him without saying a word. Arland continued, "So then, if that's a possible explanation for the first two incidents . . . . then wouldn't it follow that, similarly, another blood clot caused yesterday's ischemic incident . . . but this time it went to Fran's brain instead of to her heart . . . but since it was a smaller clot like the first one, it didn't leave any permanent damage?"

The doctor stood silently in the doorway, shuffling his weight back and forth from one foot to the other while staring at his shoes. After a few moments he walked closer to Arland and said, "Well, Mr. Dwelle . . . I can't say for sure . . . but yes . . . yes, it *is* a possibility that all three of these incidents could have been caused by blood clots . . . yes, it's a real possibility . . . I think we'll look into this . . . and when we know something more, I'll get back to you." And with a quick nod of thanks, he turned and left the room.

Arland plopped down on the chair beside my bed, emotionally spent from his volley of questions. For the rest of that day and into the night, he turned over and over in his mind every detail of the previous days, searching for the missing piece that would solve the puzzle of my health problems.

What Arland didn't know, however, was that he had actually found the missing piece! His desperate quest for answers had brought him, unknowingly, to the periphery of a new frontier in blood research, a medical terrain explored by only a handful of doctors in the world. And the doctors making these groundbreaking discoveries worked in—of all places—the city of Vienna, Austria! Of course, Arland didn't know that either. He had never heard of them or their work. And none of them had ever heard of me, a patient named Frances Dwelle.

At least, not yet.

# Day Twenty-Five

Ten days after the second heart attack, the doctors tried to wean me off the life support machines, but my heart still showed no improvement. They also tried having me do some exercises, but I wasn't strong enough to do even the simplest ones.

During this time, visits by dear friends would brighten my days. Greg and Sandie came nearly every day—sometimes, together, but often, separately. Each visit gave me a huge emotional boost as we talked about our church, chatted and laughed together, and prayed for our families. Often, Sandie would bring me a scrumptious dish she had prepared, like a piece of grilled steak, or buy me a decadent treat like a Mars ice cream bar. She and Greg stopped by our home daily to check on the welfare of the girls. Sandie was also Jessi's confidante and helped her deal with my illness.

I asked Sandie for an update on the recent JOY International breakfast I had missed. Responding with her typical enthusiasm, she said, "Fran, it was such a wonderful morning! The hotel ballroom, the meal, and the music were all spectacular! Over two hundred women were there from different nations and religious backgrounds, including refugees from the Balkan war. Our speaker challenged the women to experience for themselves how Christ gives joy and hope in even the most difficult times. At the end, during the *table-talk* time, there was a lot of lively discussion and positive responses from the women."

I was thrilled to hear her report. When she finished, I added, "And now, Sandie, look at my situation today. *I'm* the one who's facing the most challenging time of *my* life. I could have never imagined this happening when we started JOY International six months ago."

Dr. Melvin was another person who often checked in on me. Several times a week, he would skip his lunch hour and take public transportation across town from the *AKH* to the *Wilhelminenspital*. He would touch base with us and answer any questions we had about my heart problems. And Arland had a million of them! Dr. Melvin also talked to the attending physicians every time he came. He said the reason he came to Vienna was because the care and research here were of the highest caliber. He always had a smile on his face, yet he could not totally hide his distress over my lack of improvement. Early on, he had made it clear that he felt a heart transplant was my only hope, but I would not even talk to him about it. Perhaps, by refusing to consider it, I only added to the disappointment he already felt.

Arland found emotional support from friends who came to the hospital. Greg and Bobby, our colleagues in missions service, were mainstays for him. Both had demanding travel schedules, Greg in Central Europe, and Bobby in the Balkan countries. Yet, they often came to the hospital and waited in a "commons" area, sitting for hours on uncomfortable, cast-iron radiators lined around the perimeter of the room. By their presence, they reminded Arland every day that he was not alone.

Danny and Ginger also visited regularly, always coming separately. Danny brought me news about people in the church, read from the Bible, and prayed for me. Ginger massaged my feet with lotions, styled my hair with a curling iron, and brought me flowers and magazines. During one visit we talked about our recent Bible study on knowing God's true character which is often different from our distorted perceptions of Him. That study deepened my capacity to trust in His character, especially His love, faithfulness, and goodness. I said to Ginger, "I never imagined then that it was equipping me for this." She laughed and said, "Neither did I."

On another visit she remarked, "Fran, I think this room is quite ugly. Why don't we do something to brighten this place up?" I laughed and said, "Well, what do you expect, Ginger? After all, it *is* a hospital, not a hotel. Maybe at least we could hang a poster or two on the wall," I suggested. So, her friend made a large, bright pink poster with one of my favorite Scripture verses on it, and we hung it up. Ginger also helped provide care for Cami and did fun things with her, like going to McDonalds.

Other friends brightened my dull days. Two friends from the Filipino fellowship came every other day with a dozen yellow roses and just sat with me—not talking, just being present. Another friend offered to clean my house every week, which I gladly accepted. People in the two churches we attended brought my family meals every day for weeks. I told another friend that I had a craving for Granny Smith apples. Even though springtime was off-season for apples, she went around to one open market after another and found enough to fill a small basket. My walking partner Jeanette visited along with her husband Gerhard, pastor of the Austrian fellowship of Vienna Christian Center. Jeannette had been bothered by the thought that our rigorous walk together had caused my first heart attack. I assured her that it did not.

In addition, there was one more gift many gave me—the gift of prayer. Week after week, people from churches in Vienna, as well as churches in America and Europe, were praying for me. People I knew well, and people I had never met, were all praying for me. I'm sure this mighty groundswell of prayer was sustaining my family and me, especially in times when our own spiritual resources were depleted. Sheryl told me, "I wept, I wrestled, I centered my thoughts on your broken health while interceding for Arland, Kaci, Jessica and Cami. All of us in the Dwelle-family-support-circle felt your pain intensely, and we were determined together to trust God for your healing."

# Day Twenty-Six

D r. Steinbach gave me another positive report. He said, "It's been uphill for the last seven days," meaning my condition has been getting better (going up) day after day. He took me off the antibiotics, which was a major development. He and the other doctors had been talking about it for several days, but they were not sure if they wanted to risk it. He also reduced the diuretics and the heart medicine, and they removed the heart vein catheter. Although the doctor said my condition had stabilized, he was still very cautious as to the reasons for the improvement. He was not as urgent as before on the necessity of a transplant, but that did not mean it was no longer being considered. Just not urgent. He did not make any promises nor give much encouragement.

Later in the day we celebrated Jessica's 15th birthday. We decided to have a makeshift party in my hospital room in the ICU. In addition to Arland and Cami, the Mundis family joined us along with my parents and my sister Norene from Seattle. The nurse said we had too many people, but since it was a special occasion, she overlooked it. Sandie made a delicious birthday cake. For two hours we shared stories and laughed. At times we were so loud I thought the nurse might come in and shut the party down. She never did. Perhaps she, too, was glad to hear joyful sounds coming from my room. We gave Jessi the Student Bible and an Esprit sport outfit for her birthday gifts. She and Cami especially enjoyed this party. For a few hours, at least, it took the edge off the sadness they were carrying over my illness.

# Day Twenty-Nine

Two weeks after my second heart attack, I was moved out of ICU into a room in the cardiac care unit. The young doctor who had told Arland I might not survive another night returned that day from her time off. At the start of her shift, she immediately came to my room. Walking in with a smile, she said in perfect English, "Mrs. Dwelle, I am *so* pleased to learn how you've been doing. What a surprise this is!" It was obvious from her amazement that she had wondered if I would even be alive when she got back.

Later that day, they took an ultrasound test of my heart. The doctor reported, "Your heart is slightly improved, but only slightly. It's still not well. Not at all." He sounded disappointed at the results.

I was far more disappointed.

That evening my parents and my sister Norene visited me. Dad and Mom came to say goodbye. Before leaving, Dad prayed a wonderful prayer, asking God to comfort, help and strengthen me. Saying goodbye to them was an emotionally wrenching experience for me, not knowing when—or if—I would see them again. Since Arland was taking them to the airport in the morning, he also left to spend the night at home. It was the first night he had not stayed with me in the hospital.

After a long day of disappointment and farewells, I was weary and my spirits were low. In the dark, I asked again, *Why Lord?* But there was no answer. *How long, Lord?* Still no answer. Yet, I knew my hope was in the Lord. . . even in the dark.

# Day Thirty-Three

My sister Norene spent her last day in Vienna visiting me before flying back home to Seattle, Washington. Her time with me and my family had been a huge encouragement. She helped my parents navigate life in a foreign culture during their time in Vienna. She stayed with my daughters in the evening and visited me every day in the hospital, often for hours at a time. She lifted my spirits by engaging me in conversations about our childhood, our families, and our mutual love for God. She boosted my faith everyday by praying and reading the Bible to me.

Norene was intrigued by the poster of Psalm 28:7 that Ginger had hung on my wall: "The Lord is my strength and my shield / My heart trusts in Him, and I am helped / My heart leaps for joy and I will give thanks to him in song." She asked, "Fran, have you really experienced joy during this trial?"

I replied, "Yes, and I'm so thankful for this. Even though I don't feel joyful about my physical condition, I'm finding that I still can rejoice in *who God is*. I have a deep-rooted joy in His love, faithfulness, and goodness."

"What other Scriptures have helped you during this time?" she asked.

"Oh, so many! Psalm 46:1 is one I have hung onto a lot: 'God is our refuge and strength, an ever-present help in trouble. Therefore, we will not fear.' Proverbs 18:10 has also been a lifeline for me: 'The name of the Lord is a strong tower; the righteous run to it and are safe.' And if I had one favorite word in these verses, it has to be the word is. I am comforted in the reminder that the Lord is my strength, is my refuge, is my strong tower and is always present to help. These three verses first became important to me in the years we lived in Zagreb. They helped me trust in God's character and tap into His strength for the day-to-day stresses we faced."

Norene said, "Fran, I know a little about your life in Zagreb, but I'd like to hear more. What were some of the challenges you faced?"

"Before I get into all that, it might be helpful to remind you why we went to Yugoslavia in the first place. Since our college days, both Arland and I had felt called to spend our lives sharing the love of Christ with others. And, as you know, we did that for a time in the States, establishing new churches. But after a while, we felt we wanted to live out that calling somewhere else besides America, somewhere in a culture different from ours. So, that's why we came to Yugoslavia."

"Was that a difficult adjustment to make?" Norene asked.

"I was surprised by how much the culture shock overwhelmed me. After all, we had received much preparation for what we would face in a different culture. Not a day passed during the first few months when I didn't have to deal with culture shock in some way. Because I didn't know the language, even a little thing—like shopping—all of a sudden became a very big thing. It was one of the activities I dreaded the most. It intimidated me because I didn't know the names of the foods. Often, I would find myself on the verge of tears, pointing and stammering in embarrassment, as I tried to just make myself understood at the open market.

"Also, for the first time in my life I experienced a nagging loneliness. I was disconnected from relationships with people outside of my family. Before Zagreb, I had rarely ever been lonely. I was blessed with many friends and was always around people. But overnight, all that drastically changed when we moved to Yugoslavia. I found myself totally separated from everything familiar—language, culture, close friends, family, foods, shopping, school—you name it! To add to the isolation, we didn't have a telephone because of a two-year wait list.

"And there were many other things that added to the stress. Things like trying to get doctors' exams and shots for a baby in a whole new medical system. Or things like washing clothes in a bathtub because there wasn't a washing machine anywhere to buy. Or things like Arland's tense and frequent interviews by the security police to extend our visa. Or things like wondering if we were under surveillance because we were foreigners in a communist country. Or things like living with a 24-hour electricity blackout every third day that left us with no heat, lights, or hot water during winter days. Or things like worrying about the ill health effects of living under a radioactive cloud from the Chernobyl nuclear power plant explosion."

Norene asked, "So, how did your girls handle being in a different culture?"

"Probably one of the most difficult things was seeing the challenges my two older daughters faced in school. They were thrown into a totally foreign system of education—Kaci in sixth grade and Jessi in first—with knowing only a few words of the Croatian language. I was deeply saddened to see how stressful school was for them. They had no support system besides immediate family, unlike now when they have friends to help them deal with my trauma. When we noticed that they began to complain a lot, even about gray buildings, we made a family rule of not complaining but giving thanks instead. That simple change of habit made a remarkable difference for us all.

"A Croatian college student named Marina was a God-send to our family. She explained many things about the Yugoslavian culture, tutored the girls and us in Croatian language studies, taught us the names of foods so we could confidently shop in the market, and assisted us in finding a doctor, dentist and piano teacher."

"So then," Norene asked, "how was it possible to handle all these daily stresses without becoming totally exhausted and overwhelmed yourself?"

"I had no other option--I *had* to trust God. I *had* to remain strong each day; I *had* to maintain my spiritual and emotional equilibrium—if for no other reason—just so I could help my daughters! And the sustaining factor for me in everything was relying on God's strength for each day. A favorite promise was 'My grace is sufficient for you, for my power is made perfect in weakness.' (2 Cor. 12:9) When I first left the States, a friend gave me a bookmark which said, 'God will never lead you where His grace cannot keep you.'

"Eventually, my Croatian language skills improved, I adjusted to the new culture, formed good friendships, and began to see the fulfillment of our purpose for being there. Three and a half years later, when the authorities revoked our visa, we moved to Vienna, but felt sad leaving friends and the life we knew in Yugoslavia."

Norene said, "So it seems pretty clear that those years in Zagreb prepared you for what you're now having to face. Right?"

"Without a doubt," I said. "Yes, for sure!"

Before saying goodbye, Norene prayed a blessing for me based on one of her favorite Scriptures: "Cast your cares on the Lord and he will sustain you; he will never let the righteous fall." (Psalm 55:22).

It was a Scripture I would cling to again and again in the coming weeks.

# Day Thirty-Eight

After three weeks in ICU and CCU, I was finally able to get out of bed and walk a little. But it was only a little. The nurses monitored my steps—first ten baby steps, then twenty—like a toddler. They were also able to wean me off the machines. Since I had a tiny bit of improvement, I asked Dr. Steinbach, "When can I go home? Just let me see how I can do." But he was against the idea. Day after day, I persisted, "Please let me go home. I can do everything there that I do here. Arland can monitor my blood pressure and my heart. And since I only live ten minutes from the hospital, I can easily get back here if there are any problems. Besides, I have young children at home who need their mother." Reluctantly, he finally released me for a few days so I could see what kind of home life I would have with congestive heart failure.

Sadly, I saw I didn't have much of a life at all. When I first got home, it took me fifteen minutes to walk up the twelve steps into the front door of my house. Arland had to bring out a chair for me. I would take one step and then sit down for a minute to rest. I did this repeatedly until I got to the top step. Inside, it was the same when I walked across a room—a few steps and sit down to rest . . . repeatedly. I had no strength at all. I could not prepare even one meal. I could not do one bit of housework. I could not wash any laundry. I could not take a bath. I could hardly dress myself. Arland had to help me do everything. I was living the life of an invalid.

After three days at home, my lungs filled with fluid, making it difficult to breathe. So, I returned to the hospital for two days. They put me back on machines that gave me heart stimulants and drained fluid from my lungs. After two days of this, I felt much better, so I was allowed to go back home. But three days later, I had to return to the hospital for the same treatment. This pattern was repeated over and over.

During all this time, there was absolutely no improvement in my condition. To make matters worse, my heart was working too poorly to supply enough oxygen to my brain. As a result, I could not get any sleep, leaving me exhausted all the time. Often during the long night hours, I asked, "Why Jesus? You visited me. You touched my body, so I didn't die. Why can't you come again and complete the healing of my heart?" But He was silent. I knew He was there because I could feel His presence and comfort, but He was not speaking to me in any tangible way.

Occasionally, I would succumb to discouragement, especially when I saw the toll the illness was taking on my family. Arland was totally exhausted—all the time. He had not had a good night's sleep for days, going into weeks. His eyes were red, and his face was drawn from the constant strain. The sight of my helpless condition had left my daughters wondering if their mother was going to live or die.

Jessi was fourteen when I became ill. She wrote an essay for school describing what life was like for us during this time. Here is an excerpt:

> *Over the next month, Mom's life hung on a thread.*
> *One by one the fibers tore, but the thread didn't break.*
> *Mom just kept swinging, back and forth, back and forth.*

Jessi soon reached a point where she felt she couldn't take it anymore. She wrote in another essay: *I only have two alternatives. I can choose to trust God, or I can choose to despair. One leads to life, the other to hopelessness.*

Some mornings when I woke up discouraged—*not another day of this, will it ever end, how much longer*—I found that I *could* make the choice my daughter had written about. I could choose to trust rather than to despair.

One day, when I was sitting on the couch in a lethargic state, Cami came into the room with her small pink Bible in her hand. She asked, "Mommy, is the Bible always true?"

I said, "Yes, it *is* always true."

Then she asked, "Does God always answer prayer?"

"Yes, He does, but not always in the way we're asking for."

"Well, you're going to walk again, Mommy. I found this verse in the Bible that says just that."

"Okay, Cami, show me the verse."

She said, "It's Isaiah 40:31. It says, 'They that wait upon the Lord will renew their strength. They will mount up with wings as eagles. They will run and not be weary; they will walk and not faint.' I know you're going to walk again, Mommy." She pointed to the Vienna Woods across the street and said, "I know you're going to walk again in those woods." She was totally convinced because God's Word had built up faith in her heart. And I, too, was encouraged by her faith.

That verse spoke about *waiting* for the Lord. I felt like I had spent a long period of time in "God's waiting room." I was waiting for God to renew my strength. I was waiting for God to help me live a normal life again. I was waiting for God to heal my heart. But there was no change. Day after day, God was silent. I felt like I had entered into the Gospel story where Jesus was asleep in the boat while the storm was raging. The disciples asked him, "Don't you care that we're about to drown?"

Jesus responded by speaking to the storm: "Peace, be still!" His message to them was clear: *I am with you; no need to worry about the storm.*

And I realized He was responding the same way to my questions about my storm.

But why, Lord? . . . *Peace, be still! I am with you.*

But when, Lord? . . . *Peace, be still! I am with you.*

But how long, Lord? . . . *Peace, be still! I am with you.*

But what if, Lord? . . . *Peace, be still! I am with you.*

*Peace, I am.*

63

# Day Forty-Three

During this time, the doctors continued to search for the cause of my heart problems. When I was strong enough, they did an angiogram. Surprisingly, it showed no cause for concern regarding my coronary arteries. This puzzled the doctors even more. With clear arteries, they wondered what could have caused such a massive heart attack. Could it have been something other than my heart, like an embolism or a thrombosis? Arland had suggested that very possibility three weeks earlier when he asked, "Is it possible the problem is not with her heart but with her blood?"

So, they decided to check my blood. Dr. Steinbach knew of research being done at the *AKH* by Dr. Helmut Sinzinger. He and his team had identified a rare blood disorder which they named the *Wien Hietzing* Syndrome. This disorder appeared in younger women who had unexplainable heart attacks. Dr. Sinzinger had traced the cause to a defect in the platelets of the blood.

I was sent to the Department of Nuclear Medicine at the *AKH* to see him. He took twelve vials of blood and ran countless tests to see if I had this blood disorder. After several weeks, he and his team came up with an answer. They concluded that I did indeed have this rare defect in the platelets of my blood, a defect that causes blood clots to form spontaneously. He had identified the problem as a defective prostaglandin receptor which disposes the platelets to clumping or coagulation. When this happens, he hypothesized, the clump or clot can clog a coronary artery, and the heart can be irreparably damaged. Afterwards, the clog itself often dissolves spontaneously so that there's no smoking gun, no evidence of what happened. This extremely rare condition is what caused my two heart attacks. In order to prevent it from ever happening again, I was put on a very unsophisticated drug regimen—one baby aspirin a day!

Only three medical teams in the world had done any research on this problem, and two of them had done only minimal testing. But the Vienna team had done extensive research, including the publishing of their findings in medical journals. Arland and I were amazed at God's providential wisdom and provision for me. I was far from America, suffering with an extremely rare blood disorder, and the only lab in the world doing major research on this condition was located in the city where I lived—Vienna, Austria!

The Vienna doctors confirmed what Arland had suspected early on: my heart was never the problem; my blood was the problem. So, the question for the doctors—what caused the two "heart attacks"—finally had been answered: my healthy heart had been destroyed by my unhealthy blood!

Now I had only one question left—and this one was for God. How long must I wait for You to heal my heart?

# Day Forty-Eight

On a beautiful Sunday afternoon, Arland took me out of the house for a walk in the park. We wanted to see what quality of life I could experience in my present condition before seriously considering a heart transplant. We went to *Kongress Park*, one of Vienna's many meticulously landscaped parks. Stately sycamore trees and blooming rose bushes line a 12-foot-wide pebbled path that goes around the park. Normally, it would take me five minutes to walk that perimeter. On this day, however, I could only shuffle my feet slowly—one step every few seconds—along the relatively flat surface. Every 20-25 feet, I would need to sit down on one of the wooden benches and rest for a minute. Wherever there was the slightest incline—one too small for a normal person to notice—I would have extreme difficulty making it up that tiny slope.

On that day, my walk in the park took 45 minutes, not 5 minutes. When it was over, I was hit forcefully with the reality that my heart was very weak. *Very* weak. A one-year-old toddler could have walked that park faster than I did. Until that time, I had been thinking, *Well, it doesn't really matter what the doctors are saying because I'm going to keep getting stronger and stronger.* Arland, also, was alarmed after that outing. It confirmed his worst fears—that *if* I survived, I would never have much of a life at all.

When we got back home, Arland said, "Honey, I'm taking you back tomorrow morning to the hospital."

"No, Arland. Please, no." I started crying and then moaning. Sobbing hurt so much I would hunch my back, rocking back and forth to the rhythm of my moaning.

"Fran, it's been two days; you have to go back."

"No, I can't go back there again. Don't make me go back, I dislike it so much, Arland."

"We have no choice, Honey. Your lungs are filling with water and your body is showing edema again. You can't wait another day. You need to get back on the heart stimulants and diuretics to drain the fluid from your lungs."

I knew Arland was right, but I dreaded going back to the hospital. For one thing, I didn't want to be away from my daughters and home. Also, I still fretted over my limited ability with the German language. Would I be able to adequately speak my concerns? Would I understand important points that were communicated to me? Dialogue with my attending physicians was never an issue because every doctor who cared for me spoke English, most of them fluently. However, I worried about my interaction with the other staff. Before going back to the hospital each time, I always prayed, "God, please help me to not have any language barriers." God answered my prayer, and I was always able to communicate in my low-to-intermediate-level German with the nurses. Still, I always felt uncertain, not knowing what to expect and not sure if everything was okay. On one occasion, I was inadvertently given medication that could have endangered my life had I not recognized—in my weakened state—that the dosage was wrong.

Another concern I had was that there were few dietary restrictions. I rarely received fish, chicken or turkey; normally, it was beef or pork. Often the dinner was cold sausage and hard cheese with bread, salad drenched in heavy mayo, or bologna strips in marinated cream sauce. After several weeks of these meals, I expressed my concerns to Dr. Steinbach. "The food I'm being served seems very unhealthy for someone struggling with a heart condition. High in cholesterol. High in fat. Does the hospital have a dietician who can plan special meals for people like me with heart issues?"

His response was very matter-of-fact. "That's just how the *Wilhelminenspital* is," he said. "It's in the 16th District of the city, the area where people eat hearty food and lots of sausage. So, the Viennese people love the food at our hospital. It's like home-cooked Austrian food. And we'd be out of business," he joked, "if we didn't serve this kind of robust food. So—the answer is no. We do not have a dietician to provide low-fat, low-cholesterol meals for you." He was implying since it was not a concern to them, it shouldn't concern me either. But I decided, just for my own peace of mind, to avoid eating such high-cholesterol food when my heart was operating at only 25% capacity. Instead, I usually gave most of my meal to Arland. However, there was one "meal" I loved and never missed--the Austrian mid-afternoon *Jause* of cake and coffee.

So, on several levels, the thought of going back to the hospital was stressful to me, but I finally saw I had no other choice. My feeble walk in the park, along with my helpless condition at home, had dramatically shown me how debilitated I was.

I had only one hope left: *Please, Jesus, complete the healing You started when You visited me.*

# Day Forty-Nine

I woke up early, feeling tired because of a sleepless night. The fluid build-up in my lungs had again made it hard to breathe and sleep. I heard Jessi and Cami talking quietly as they prepared for school. I dragged myself out of bed to say good morning and hug them. I reminded them I was going to the hospital for another two-to-three days. Cami asked, "Again, Mom? Do you think they can make you better this time?"

"I hope so. We'll wait and see."

We continued chatting as we kept an eye on the clock. As they rushed to leave, I said a short prayer for them at the front door. Jessica walked down to the corner where she began a climb of 110 stairs on *Essel Stiege* (donkey stairs) to catch her bus to the English-language American International School. Cami walked 15 minutes to the neighborhood German-language Austrian school.

*They both are probably quite relieved to go off to school, I said to myself. It must be a welcome distraction from the grim reality of seeing their once-healthy mother now so weak and listless and fatigued and ashen-colored. Zombie-like, I thought. That must be how I look to them. Walking death, shuffling slowly around the house.*

Wearily, I got dressed for the day. Arland and I ate a simple breakfast before leaving for the hospital. He held my arm to stabilize me as I walked down the steps to our car. Then we slowly drove to the hospital. He had not adopted the Viennese style of driving fast and ignoring the speed limit. (Once we were stopped by a police car for driving too slowly. Our daughters laughed about this and never let him forget it.)

Along the way, I looked at some of the familiar things I loved about Vienna: the neighborhood grocery store with our favorite cheeses and crusty rolls; the coffee house with delicious dark coffee and delightful aromas; the pastel-colored houses with flowering window baskets; the bakery with *Apfelstrudel* (apple strudel), cakes and sweet rolls; the fragrant flower stands on every-other corner; the park with children playing and mothers watching and friends chatting; the park benches with people reading newspapers and elderly men playing chess; the screeching street cars and the honking autos. I noticed one elderly Austrian woman easily climbing the few steps onto a tram. I remembered how I used to do that, too, but now it was impossible.

I said, "Look, Arland. Life is going on as usual for all of them. Do you think my life will ever go back to what it was like before? Will I ever be strong and well again to do the things I enjoy?"

"Fran, I hope so. We need to keep praying, trusting the Lord, and not giving up." I thought about that for a minute. *Yes, I'm going to continue to trust God to make me strong again.*

After 20 minutes, we arrived at *Wilhelminenspital*, the hospital in the 16th district. After checking in, we walked to my room. The nurse greeted me with the standard Austrian greeting, "*Gruss Gott*," which literally translates, "May God greet you." I undressed, put on the yellow gown, and climbed into the bed. The nurse hooked me up to the machine that would stimulate my heart and drain water from my lungs.

I prepared myself for another two-to-three-day ordeal, hopin to feel stronger when it was over. To help pass the time, I focused my mind on many Scriptures that speak of God's strength. Isaiah 41:10 became one of my favorites: "So do not fear, for I am with you; do not be dismayed, for I am your God. I will strengthen you and help you; I will uphold you with my righteous right hand."

Discouraged by my physical infirmity, I needed God's word to strengthen my spirit as much as I needed heart stimulants to strengthen my body.

72

# Day Fifty

D r. Melvin came on his lunch hour to visit. He wanted to know how my three days at home had gone. Arland told him about my "walk" in the park and how discouraging it was. Dr. Melvin said, "Unfortunately, you can expect more of that."

"But she feels so good after she's been put back on the intravenous heart stimulants and diuretics," Arland said, "and they drain the water out of her system."

"True," Dr. Melvin said, "but you cannot expect that to go on forever. The stabilization these treatments gave her right after her second heart attack definitely saved her from certain death. That was wonderful, of course; it strengthened her enough to survive. But it did not offer any hope of improvement nor any hope for long-term stabilization. The minute she's disconnected from the heart stimulation machine, her lungs will start filling with fluid, the edema will start again, and she'll have to return to the hospital for another treatment. So, yes, this cycle of going-home-and-coming-back-for-stimulation is helping for now, but every time she's hooked up to that machine, her heart is weakened a little more. Her time at home between treatments will start becoming shorter and shorter because her heart is in a relentless downward cycle. Its endurance cannot continue like this indefinitely."

Dr. Melvin stopped there. He didn't have to spell out for Arland what the next stage was in my downward cycle. Arland knew quite well: congestive heart failure—I would either die, or I would be an invalid for the rest of my life. There were no other possible outcomes. Unless . . .

Unless—as Dr. Melvin strongly believed—I agreed to have a heart transplant. He talked to Arland about it. "I don't know if it's even in the realm of possibility for Fran to get a transplant, but if it is, I'm guessing she would have a long wait for an organ. In that case, maybe a mechanical assist device could keep her heart working while she waited."

Arland said, "Well, as you already know, Fran is not ready to consider getting a heart transplant. But I'm curious to know anyway—how would such a heart device work?" Dr. Melvin launched into a detailed description of the different kinds of mechanical devices, including the pros and cons of each. When he was done, Arland said, "Dr. Melvin, you're obviously very passionate about this subject. What made you decide to pursue this kind of research when you were already a successful surgeon?"

"A couple reasons, I guess. First of all, I had a difficult time handling the stressful demands placed on a heart transplant surgeon—trying to juggle the available organs with the overwhelming number of people who needed them. And secondly, I realized early on there would never be enough donors. So, I gave up surgery, went back to university and got an engineering degree. Then, I started doing research to develop a workable artificial heart. I've found this work to be very fulfilling, even though it meant a great cut in salary. When I learned others in Vienna were doing similar research, I came here to be part of that process. And you're right, Arland--I *am* passionate about this. I'm passionate to find a way to help solve the heart problems that plague so many people. And, of course, that includes Fran. So, I'm here for you both . . . anytime . . . for any reason."

Dr. Melvin's concern for my health was reassuring. But I certainly did not share his passion for a machine to keep alive my almost-dead heart. I wanted neither a mechanical device nor a transplanted heart. I wanted a healed heart. From the Lord. Nothing else.

# Day Sixty-Four

Each time I came back from the hospital, my first day home was pretty good. With my blood still full of the heart stimulants, my breathing was not too labored. But this was my third day home, so by now I could hardly breathe because my lungs were filling with water. At night, I would lie in a halfway reclining position, trying to find a way to get enough air, but it was not easy to do. If I could not breathe, that meant I could not sleep; so, I would lie awake most of the night. This was one of those nights.

In my bedroom there was a large window with a cross-shaped center bar. When the streetlight shined through the window, it created a silhouette of a cross. Every night I would look at it because it was the only light in the room. And I would think about how the cross was God's greatest expression of His love. It also reminded me of Jesus praying, "Not my will but yours be done." I felt God was asking me to submit to His will and trust Him. So, I had to come to terms with this: *Can I trust you, God, even if I die?* I could honestly say, *Yes, I can trust You, because I believe You are good.*

The cross also reminded me of those who were suffering, particularly the women of Yugoslavia who were enduring the ravages of civil war. Many of them were sent to refugee camps where they were separated from families, friends, and everything familiar. I could only imagine their sorrow. On many nights I prayed for them.

I also meditated in those sleepless hours on the character of God. One particular verse that would race through my mind nightly was Proverbs 28:10—*The name of the Lord is a strong tower / The righteous run into it and they are safe.* I had learned earlier that "the name of the Lord" means His character—who He is and what He can do. So, I would praise God for His love, His goodness, His faithfulness, His wisdom, His mercy, His sovereignty . . . and so on. Through the dark hours of this night, as in many others, my sleeplessness became sweet communion with God.

Finally, morning dawned, and the cross-shadow faded away into oblivion. For a brief moment, I wondered if my body might soon do the same.

*But no! Of course not,* I suddenly thought. *After all, my God is also my Healer! He will complete the healing of my heart.* I had no doubt of this, even though I did not understand why He was silent or why the healing was delayed.

# Day Sixty-Nine

Greg asked Arland to speak at the Sunday night service at Vienna Christian Center. This church had a special place in our hearts because we had been part of the team that had started it a few years earlier. The congregation was a beautiful mix of many nationalities. Along with people at The International Chapel (where we also attended), they modeled how *the family of God* cares for one another.

When Arland stood at the pulpit that night, he looked out at the people who had showered us with a thousand kindnesses: cards, prayers, visits, flowers, and meals. (Our girls especially loved the Filipino noodle dishes.) He thanked them for being the channel through which our family experienced God's comfort. He affirmed them for the many ways they had demonstrated their faith in the midst of our crisis. He said he had learned from them that the prayers of others will carry us in difficult times when our own prayers seem deficient.

The church service began with its usual vibrant worship time, but one thing had been missing for many weeks. It was me. I was not playing the piano as I usually did for worship. Arland looked over at the grand piano and missed seeing me there. And he knew how much I missed playing, too. From the youngest age, I had played the piano almost every day of my life, but for weeks now I had not played even once. In my condition, I was too weak to press down the keys. Furthermore, I did not even have a desire to play, something I never imagined would happen to me.

Arland entitled his sermon, "He's There in the Storm." He spoke from the Book of Acts where Paul was in the middle of a storm and said, "For there stood by me this night an angel of the God to whom I belong and whom I serve, saying, 'Do not be afraid . . . (Acts 27:23).'" He shared that in the last two months he and I had both found Paul's experience to be relevant to us like never before—God stays near to us in the dark times and helps us not to fear.

However, Arland did not share the full picture of how dark those times had been for him. During the weeks after my second heart attack, he experienced this *darkness* as overwhelming emotional numbness—just putting one foot in front of the other, doing whatever had to be done in a day. He struggled coping with what we were up against as it became obvious my health crises were not going away; if anything, they were getting worse. This meant, he thought, that we were looking at the imminent approach of my death. With this pall covering everything, the best he could manage each day was simply to plod. Just plod. He became perpetually numb—physically, emotionally and spiritually—trying to handle the onslaught of crisis after crisis.

He quickly discovered that the daily requirements of life are relentless—they don't diminish just because we have more urgent concerns. On the night of my first heart attack, Arland remembered that he had not taken care of a slow leak in one of his tires. He knew that if he didn't leave the hospital room to get that tire filled, he would not be able to use his car. So, after the nurses told him my life was not in danger and they would keep me under observation, he jumped into his car and drove to the gas station. As he was kneeling on the ground filling the tire, he was overwhelmed with the incongruity of the whole situation. *This is surreal*, he thought. *Here's my wife, lying in a hospital, perhaps dying from a heart attack, and I'm out here putting air in a low tire!*

At home, Arland's days were filled with helping me get up, helping me shower, helping me get to bed, helping me do laundry, sorting out my prescriptions, and getting the girls off to school.

After six weeks, the food brigade had stopped, so he was also cooking meals. But on the other hand, those relentless demands of life—in their own way—also brought comfort to Arland. They helped *momentarily* alleviate his anxieties over my condition by giving a semblance of order and structure to his days.

Arland's career work as a missionary was impeded during this time. At the time of my crisis, he was involved in the training of pastors in former Yugoslavia and in Romania. But after a few weeks, he realized he could not care for me and our daughters and still maintain the necessary teaching demands in the seminary program. He also had been working to get Christian films translated into the Slovakian language for public showings in the former Communist country. But most of these projects were put on hold when my health failed. However, one special film project, Corrie Ten Boom's story in "The Hiding Place," had been completed just prior to my first heart attack. On Easter Sunday, while I was in the hospital, the film debuted on Slovakian television all over the country, and the response was overwhelmingly positive. Hundreds of people asked for printed materials about the Christian faith. This was a big encouragement for him in the midst of all the other heaviness he was carrying.

That Sunday night, Arland concluded his sermon by reminding the people that the same God who was *present* with Paul in his crisis would also be *present* with them in their storms. Both he and I could attest to that from our firsthand experience.

As I saw it, though, there was one difference between Paul's storm and mine. His ended after two weeks, but mine was still raging after ten weeks. I wondered, *How much longer can I hold on?* The doctors were saying . . . "Not much longer."

God was saying . . .

N.o.t.h.i.n.g.

# Day Seventy

My hospital room had a view of the *Schloss Wilhelminenberg*, a majestic white palace situated on a hill overlooking Vienna. I had often walked those palace grounds, but now it seemed impossible I would ever do that again. Every time I stood in front of the window, I prayed, *Lord, help me to walk on those grounds again.* The *Schloss* seemed like a visual reminder of my hope that God would lift me out of my medical prison.

This day, June 1, was our 24th wedding anniversary. Arland came about 5:00 p.m., carrying a wicker basket in one hand and flowers in the other. I said, "Oh, what is this?" With a smile on his face, he began emptying the basket: first a tablecloth, then candlesticks, and then—*to my delight*—carryout Chinese food, a welcome break from the daily hospital fare. He set up everything on a little table and placed it by the window. While we enjoyed our gourmet dinner by candlelight, the nurses came in and added their congratulations to our celebration.

We reminisced about past anniversaries, where we were and what we did. We talked about the future. I kept thinking, *I wonder where we'll spend our 25th anniversary.* I felt so grateful to be alive and to have the strength to enjoy Arland's company. He had been my constant companion through every day of my ordeal, showing me more care and compassion than I ever imagined a husband could do. Looking out the window at the *Schloss Wilhelminenberg*, I said,

"Next year, Arland, I want to celebrate our 25th anniversary by walking up there on those palace grounds."

We talked about immediate plans for my medical care. We simply wanted to get to the States where I could have access to the American medical system and where our family could settle. If I were still going to be in a holding pattern for heart surgery, we wanted it to be in America, not in Austria. We then spent time in prayer together, asking the Lord to restore my health and bring to pass our 25th anniversary.

I knew Arland was wondering if we would actually have another anniversary. I suspected he had thought about it all day. *Will we have a 25th and, if so, what will it be like? Will my wife be in permanent intensive care or be a homebound invalid? Or something else?* Before leaving that night, he gave me a card he had spent several hours writing. Printed in beautiful decorative script, it expressed his gratitude for our years together and his hope that we would have more.

*Fran, my Darling,*
*Today we mark twenty-four years of shared life.*
*I have been walking among gentle memories,*
*recalling the preparation for our marriage,*
*the anticipation—*
*recalling the early years of growing acquaintance and intimacy—*
*the later years when we witnessed birth*
*of children and a church—*
*the more recent years when we became*
*strangers and pilgrims*
*to obey a high call.*
*I covet more – don't leave me now.*
*HAPPY ANNIVERSARY!*

# Day Seventy-Two

I experienced another long, miserable night at home, struggling to breathe. Throughout my crisis, breathing was always more difficult at nighttime. With my heart's diminished pumping capacity, there was insufficient blood supply to the breathing control center of my brain. As a result, whenever I fell into a sound sleep, my breathing would stop—maybe for 30 seconds, or 40, or even a minute. Then suddenly I would wake up, gasping for air, hyperventilating, and coughing. These breathing "fits" disturbed Arland's sleep most of the night, too. He would lie there half-awake for hours, listening to my breathing start and stop—over and over—and listening to the rattling sounds in my lungs when I coughed. It's no wonder we both lived on the edge of exhaustion all the time!

Other times, I had to sit up in order to breathe. Arland propped pillows on top of my bedside table. I found some relief by sitting with my legs crossed, and my arms crossed on top of the pillows, and my head resting on my arms. But staying in that position all night long caused leg cramps and back pain. Also, as soon as I fell into a deep sleep, I would stop breathing. Awaking in a panic, I would cry out, "Arland, I can't breathe! Help me, help me breathe! How do I do it?"

Arland then would coach me through steps of breathing: "Fran, now exhale . . . and blow out carefully . . . empty your lungs . . .

now just draw in . . . that's right, Fran . . . be calm . . . now blow out again . . . ." A simple involuntary action had become a life-and-death struggle. After ten weeks of this trauma, my breathing had worsened more than ever. I was not sure how much longer I could go on like this. I was feeling and tasting death. I could actually feel my body shutting down.

I knew all too well the feeling of death. I had tasted it before as a 10-year-old girl, drowning in the dark cold waters of a stone quarry on a warm summer afternoon. I had gone that day to the abandoned quarry across from our house with my younger siblings—Norene, age 9, and Mark, age 7. We were throwing rocks into the water to see who could throw them the farthest. I got too close to the shoreline and fell into the water. I stood up, took one step and fell into a deep pit of water. I didn't realize that the bottom of a quarry does not have a gradual descent like a lake has. Rather, its bottom is jagged and uneven and drops off abruptly.

Instantly, I panicked. I couldn't breathe! I couldn't swim! I knew I was drowning! I prayed in desperation, "Jesus, save me! Jesus, help me!"

My brother and sister were frantic. Norene ran home as fast as she could and shouted out to my parents who were napping, "Frances is drowning! Frances is drowning!"

My mother and father immediately got up and began running to the quarry. My father didn't even put on his shoes but ran barefoot, crying and praying all the way, "Jesus, save her! Jesus, save her!"

My little brother stood on the shore in total shock—unable to move or talk— watching in disbelief as I floundered. He saw me come up to the surface, arms flailing. I cried out, "Help! Help!" before sinking into the water again. I came up the second time and yelled out to him, "I'm drowning! Get help!" My cry jolted him out of his shock, and he ran off to get help.

On the other side of the quarry, two 18-year-old Eagle Scouts heard my screams of distress. Immediately, they jumped into the water and swam across the quarry to rescue me. By then, I had gone under three times, and I felt sure I was going to drown. All of a sudden, I felt their strong arms grab me and pull me up to the surface. While I gasped for air, they carried me to shore. As they laid me on the ground, I saw my father and mother running down the path towards me with tears streaming down their faces. They immediately kissed me and hugged me as they prayed between sobs, "Thank you, Jesus!"

*So Lord, I'm feeling that I'm drowning again. But this time I'm dying by heart sickness, not by water. It feels like I'm on the verge of going under for the last time. Oh God, you saved me from certain death before. You heard my cry for help as a young girl, and you rescued me! So now, I'm crying out to you once more: Jesus, help me! Jesus, save me! I'm putting all my trust in you. Let your word be fulfilled in my life once again: "He reached down from on high and took hold of me; he drew me out of the deep waters."* (Psalm 18:16)

Thankfully, I awoke—if ever I slept—to a new morning. Arland was already up—if ever he slept. After getting dressed and eating breakfast, we drove back to the hospital for another three-day round of heart stimulants.

# Day Seventy-Six

On the day before Greg and Sandie returned to the States for the summer, they came to visit me one last time. My condition was worse than ever. I had had a terrible night again, unable to sleep and unable to breathe. I was so colorless and lethargic that Arland thought I looked like a mummy propped up on our living room sofa. Sandie sat close to me on the couch as we talked.

Greg and Sandie wanted to know how plans were coming for our return to the States. We talked about the options before me for surgery—either staying in Vienna or going to America. We all agreed it would be best if I returned to the States for my medical care. There I would have familiarity with the American medical system and a nearby support system of family and friends.

Arland brought Greg and Sandie up-to-speed on what he had learned in recent days about a transplant. "The first thing I did," he said, "was to contact the medical director of our missions board. I presented the idea of a transplant to him, but he was skeptical about it. 'No, a heart transplant has got to be the absolutely last possible option for your wife,' he said. 'First of all, there's a very low success rate with these things, and secondly, the prognosis for any kind of life after a transplant is very, very grim.'

"The next day, however, the medical director called me back. 'You know, Arland, I was really wrong about what I told you yesterday.

I didn't realize how far transplantation had come in the last five years. The development of a brand-new drug called cyclosporine has changed everything. People now can have a relatively successful life after a transplant.' So, he gave me the go-ahead to find out what transplant options were available in the States.

"After research, Fran and I decided that a hospital in Salt Lake City was the best place. Dr. Jim Long, a renowned surgeon, heads up their heart transplant program, and it's rated one of the finest in America. He would work out the details of getting Fran accepted into their program, but she would have to live in the hospital permanently until an organ could be obtained. He said, 'I'll tell you one thing, Mr. Dwelle, we would never allow your wife to do what they're letting her do in Vienna, going back and forth from your home to the hospital. Her condition's too critical. The only way we can be assured that she's strong enough when an organ becomes available is if she's right here in the hospital, being attended to all the time.' Dr. Long said that their program had one of the shortest waiting lists in the U.S. for donor hearts. But even so, it could still take nine months or longer for one to become available.

"However, the Salt Lake City option presents a formidable challenge for us," Arland continued. "How do we find a way to transport Fran from Austria to America? Our Missions Division looked into contracting a private medical lift, but the $40,000 cost was prohibitive. They also considered putting her on a commercial flight and had contacted a cardiologist from Michigan who was willing to donate his time to accompany her. This plan would involve hooking Fran up to a portable chest pack that would give her the same heart stimulants and medications she was getting in the hospital. The cardiologist would monitor her condition for the duration of the flight, minute by minute. *Perhaps,* if her heart was strong enough when she got on the plane, the portable pack treatments might keep it strengthened all the way to Salt Lake City. But this option is risky. Once over the Atlantic, if Fran had a medical crisis, it would mean an almost certain death.

"Fran told the Vienna doctors here that she would prefer to be in America if she had to have a transplant. They were not opposed to the idea; in fact, they were very open to it. But they said she was too weak to make such a long trip. Even when we told them about the private medical escort, they insisted they would not release her until she was stronger—strong enough to breathe on her own, strong enough to sit up in a seat, strong enough to endure the rigors of a transcontinental flight. So, in a nutshell, that's where everything stands right now," Arland concluded. "We're just focused on one thing: getting Fran strong enough so she can get on a plane home to America."

When Arland finished his update, he and Greg and Sandie talked back and forth about the options before us. I sat there in silence, too weary to re-hash everything. Finally, Sandie asked, "Fran, what are your feelings about all this?"

I said, "I don't know if I can handle going to Salt Lake City. It's a big minus for me—staying in the hospital for up to a year without going home and being totally out of touch with my children." I started crying. "It all seems so hopeless, Sandie. And one more thing, what do we do with our girls' schooling? We would be uprooting them from this culture and thrusting them into another unfamiliar setting, including new schools. I just can't fathom the emotional turmoil of doing that to Jessica and Cami."

At the end of the evening, Greg served us all communion. Then he finished with a prayer, asking God to heal my heart. Then the four of us shared long embraces and said our goodbyes.

As Sandie left our house, she was overwhelmed by the hopelessness of my situation—either I was going to sit in a hospital for a year . . . or . . . I was going to die. She went out to the car and broke down weeping, wondering if her goodbye to me was our final goodbye.

And I also cried, wondering the same thing.

# Day Seventy-Nine

After six weeks of back-and-forth from home to hospital, the doctors insisted with more urgency that I needed a transplant. Dr. Guenther Laufer, particularly, encouraged me to consider it. But I held to my resolve: "No, I'm not at all interested." Every other day or so, one of them would come in and ask again. And I would repeat again, "No, let's just wait a little longer and see if things change." I was hoping God would complete my healing or—if He didn't—that some new drug or invention would get me out of this hopeless pit of congestive heart failure.

My friend, Myrna Alexander, said to me, "Fran, you're in the pit now. When you finally get to the bottom, tell us what you've found." As I watched my health slowly deteriorate, more and more each day, I could feel that I was nearing the bottom of the pit.

Finally, I decided maybe—just maybe—I should be more open to the possibility of a heart transplant. Not only were the doctors urging me to do this, but so was Arland, Greg, Sandie, and Dr. Melvin. But I had decided that if I was going to consider a transplant, I absolutely wanted it to be in America, not in Austria. Arland was in regular contact with the Salt Lake City transplant doctors, and they were ready to go. However, the Vienna doctors held firm in their insistence that I was far too weak to survive such a long trip.

So, I was in a quandary. Salt Lake City was possibly available to me, but I could not physically get there. Vienna was definitely available to me, but I did not want major surgery in a foreign hospital. The only viable option I could see was for God to complete the healing of my damaged heart.

So . . . I waited.

However, every day I waited I sank a little deeper in my proverbial pit. I was discouraged at times, but somehow, I was at peace and filled with hope. Years earlier, I had heard what Corrie Ten Boom said about *being in a pit,* and often I found myself reflecting on her words: "No pit is so deep that God is not deeper still."

Our two pits—Corrie's and mine—were vastly different: hers, a Nazi death camp, and mine, an almost dead heart. But our God was one and the same—He was Lord of the Pit.

# Day Eighty-Three

'M rs. Dwelle, I know others here at the hospital have talked to you about the possibility of a heart transplant, so I've come today to see if you've thought any more about it."
I cringed at the thought of *another* transplant talk.

"Yes, I've given it some thought," I said to the young woman doctor, "but no, I'm not ready for something that drastic yet. I'm still waiting to see if my heart's going to get stronger."

"So, you're still waiting for improvement, are you?" she asked in flawless English.

"Well, yes. One reason is because I've heard that if there's just 10% improvement in my heart's pumping efficiency—from 25% to 35%— I would have much less problem with fluids building up. Then, at least I could sleep at night. And if I could get to 50% capacity, well then it is possible—right?—for some people to live a fairly normal life with only 50% heart capacity? So yes, I *am* still waiting for my heart to get better, even if it's just a little. But if there's not any improvement, I'm still hoping maybe there's something else that can be done besides a transplant."

"Like what, Mrs. Dwelle? We've done everything that can be done. I don't know of anything else."

"How about different heart stimulants?" I asked. "Every time I come back here for another round of stimulants, I feel stronger for a day or two. But I was wondering if there was another stimulant that would work even better than what we're now using. Something that would strengthen me for a longer period of time?"

"No," she said, shaking her head. "You are already on the most potent stimulant available. It's the best one there is. But it'll never do enough to give you any hope for a normal life. Sure, if all you had to do was stay in a hospital bed and walk down the hallway once or twice a day, then these stimulants might be enough for that kind of life. But as you've already discovered, this medication cannot give you enough strength to maintain a full life. Not a life of caring for your family, your household and your normal daily routines. At best, you'll always be just one step away from becoming an invalid."

I went quiet for a few moments before saying, "I know what you mean about not being able to live a normal life. That's always the single most discouraging part of going home—seeing how little I *can* do. But I guess I've still been hoping that I can continue on this regimen—going home for a day or two, coming back here for stimulants and fluid removal, going home again—until we can find a permanent solution."

The doctor moved closer to the bed, and taking my hand in hers, said slowly, "Mrs. Dwelle, there is no other *permanent* solution. A new heart is your only hope for *permanent* health. Nothing else can stop the further deterioration of your bodily systems. Nothing . . . not even these heart stimulants."

I didn't say anything, silently praying, *Lord, I still believe You have another way. You can heal my heart. After all, that's what I have been praying for. And that's what everyone else has been praying for weeks now. Lord, why would they keep praying so faithfully unless You were energizing their prayers? Isn't it because You intend to do the healing?* I composed my thoughts and said, "Well, Doctor, I don't know what to say. I just don't know. Maybe you're right, but that's just hard for me to accept right now."

The doctor was pensive for a few moments and then said, "Okay, tell you what, Mrs. Dwelle, I want to show you something. I'd like for you to get out of bed and go with me for a short walk down the hall. Are you up for that?"

"Yes, I think so. Let me get my robe and shoes on."

Several minutes later I was ready. The doctor explained, "I'm going to take you into the heart-and-kidney ward. All the women there have very bad hearts, and a few have had heart attacks. I'll introduce you to the women there, but I want you to particularly notice the woman in bed #3. Do you know which bed that is?"

"Yes, I know how they're numbered."

"Good. We'll only stay a few minutes and then we'll come back here and talk." When we walked into the room, the doctor introduced me in German to the eight patients, all middle-aged to elderly women. I greeted each one, taking special note of the woman in bed #3. I had seen her on several occasions walking in the hallway. She always had her hair done up and wore full make-up, earrings, and jewelry. She was strikingly beautiful except for one thing—she had a huge stomach. On her slight frame, the watermelon stomach made her look like she was nine months pregnant.

When we walked back out into the hallway, the doctor asked, "Did you notice that woman in bed #3?"

"Yes, I've seen her before."

"Did you notice her stomach?"

"Yes, of course. What's wrong with her? Does she have a tumor or something?"

"No, she has that stomach because of congestive heart failure due to the buildup of bodily fluids. She either can't get a transplant, or she refuses to get one. Because her kidneys aren't functioning, she's in very critical condition right now. She won't live that way much longer."

"So, why did you want me to see her?"

The doctor stopped right there in the middle of the hallway and turned to face me. Pointing to my chest and looking me right in the eye, she said, "Mrs. Dwelle, that's exactly what you're going to look like *very soon* if you don't get a transplant."

I was startled, even somewhat frightened, by her confrontational look and urgent tone of voice. By the time we got back to the room, I was shaking inside. I asked her, "How much longer before I reach the stage where that woman's at?"

"I can't say for sure," she answered. "But probably sooner than you think."

"What makes you say that?"

"Because you've been thinking that your health situation is static—not getting better, not getting worse—and that you can still function day after day, even if it's only in a weakened state. But that's simply not true. The tests we've done already show that your kidneys are failing. Soon it will be your lungs. Since your heart's not pumping enough blood, your body is steadily deteriorating. Each day a little more than the day before."

I struggled to find words to say. "Well . . . I'm not sure . . . but um . . . okay . . . okay I guess maybe I should . . . I mean it'd probably be a good idea if I talked to Dr. Laufer."

"So, do you want me to contact him?" she asked?

"Yes, I think I'm ready to talk to him."

"That's good, Mrs. Dwelle. I'll go right now and see if I can reach him." A few minutes later she came back into the room and said, "Dr. Laufer will try to come by tonight to talk with you."

When Arland arrived later that afternoon, I told him about the woman with the watermelon stomach and what the doctor had said to me. He understood better than I did how critical my condition had become, yet he was still shaken by this latest revelation. "Fran, I think this means that we've run out of options. The hospital's been saying all along that you need a transplant. And you know, Dr. Melvin and Greg and Sandie all feel the same way. I, too, have been leaning that way, but now I've finally come to agree with them all. So, I'm behind you one hundred percent in your decision to talk with Dr. Laufer."

All evening long, while waiting for Dr. Laufer to come, we talked and prayed together. Finally, when we realized he was not coming, I urged Arland to go home and get a desperately needed night of rest.

But for Arland, *rest* would have to wait. At least for one more night . . . and one more day. He still had unfinished business to tend to. There could be no rest . . . until . . .

He prayed.

# Day Eighty-Four

Late that night, while tossing sleeplessly in bed, Arland realized he had not *personally* had an extensive time of prayer for my healing. He and I had prayed together often, and he and others had prayed together often, but he had been too busy for any kind of intense prayer by himself. After all, his days had been consumed with taking care of me, contacting doctors, doing medical research, helping our daughters, keeping up the home—cooking, cleaning, shopping, and laundry. With so many practical details needing attention, he felt too distracted to even think much about prayer. Moreover, the daily demands on his emotional and physical energy had left him spiritually numb. Weary to the bone, he found it almost impossible to face up to the questions that were always looming just at the edge of his consciousness: *What if my wife doesn't get better—how can we continue this way if she's incapacitated for years? What if she becomes a total invalid—how can we remain in Austria? What will I do for a career if I cannot continue my missionary service? What if Fran doesn't make it—how can I live without her? How can my girls survive without her?*

Arland felt no guilt about his inability to pray because he knew others were doing the praying. And that was comforting to him. He never felt alone; instead, he always sensed that there were arms underneath him. He felt that the prayers of God's people were sustaining him. But suddenly—on this night—he had an urgent sense that the time had come for him to do his own praying. Earnest praying. Desperate praying.

So, starting in the early morning hours and continuing throughout that day and the next, he fasted and prayed and wept for my healing. He unburdened his soul to God, spelling out his petitions and asking for divine help in ways he had never done before in my twelve-week ordeal.

At the end of that time, he sensed a release in his spirit—he had finally done it! He had verbalized his unutterable anguish to the One who could understand it fully. He had carried his crushing weight of concern to God's throne of grace. Now he was done; there was nothing more left to do. He had raised questions, he had probed for answers, he had challenged decisions, he had sought opinions, he had monitored vitals, he had kept vigils, he had consoled, he had comforted, he had torn out his hair, he had beat back despair, he had flailed at the dark. And finally . . .

Finally . . . he had prayed.

Arland *himself* had prayed.

And God was listening.

# Day Eighty-Five (1)

D
r. Laufer finally came by the next day, three days after he had first been contacted. He greeted Arland and me with his usual Austrian formalities. "Hello again, Mr. and Mrs. Dwelle; it's good to see you." Then he shook each of our hands. Since his visit involved a sensitive life-and-death discussion, he came without his normal entourage of doctors and medical students. Instead, just the head doctor, the head nurse, and one other doctor accompanied him.

He began by saying, "Since we met some weeks ago, I understand that you've given more thought to the possibility of a heart transplant."

"Yes, we think we're ready to sign up for one," Arland said, "but first we want to know more about what's involved."

"And how about you, Mrs. Dwelle? Are you yourself ready to do this?" Dr. Laufer asked.

"Well, everyone tells me it's what I need to do. I still have lots of reservations and lots of questions, but maybe they'll get taken care of after talking with you."

"Well, let's hope so," Dr. Laufer said. "Let me start by saying that I believe a transplant offers the best hope for your long-term survival. But I want to make sure you understand all the ramifications of such a surgery. So, I'm going to explain the procedure for securing an organ. Then I'll talk about the side-effects from the medications as well as any potential complications that could arise. And I'm going to deliberately paint the worst-case scenario so that you know all the risks involved."

Arland took out his pen and little black book to make notes.

Dr. Laufer continued, "The heart transplant program here in Vienna is part of the Euro-Transplant Foundation, an organ registration service for West European countries. It's a database in which participating transplant hospitals both contribute and receive organs as they become available. Because of the scarcity of organs, this mutual sharing service helps prevent the waste of available organs by screening applications from a wider area than just one country. You'll be encouraged to know that organ availability is greater here in Europe than in the States, when all things are taken into consideration."

"Why is that?" Arland asked.

"Because most European countries have *implied consent* policies. The assumption here is that organs *can* automatically be harvested unless people have indicated beforehand that their wish is not to do that. In your country, it's the opposite. Unless you have prior consent from a signed donor statement, or by family permission in cases when the donor cannot sign, the organs automatically *cannot* be harvested in the States.

"When you agree to become a donor recipient, Mrs. Dwelle, your name will be added to the waiting list of those wanting to receive an organ. When a heart becomes available, the computer at the transplant office in The Netherlands will pick out the best candidate from the database of potential recipients."

"How is that determined?" Arland asked.

"Well, there are a number of considerations. The computer first compares compatible weight, body size and blood type of the recipient with the donor. Other things then are factored in such as age, overall health of the recipient, length of time on the waiting list and proximity of the donor organ to the recipient's location."

I asked, "Do you know where I would be on that list?"

"When I checked this morning, there were ninety-five people on the waiting list for a donor heart. Your name would go to the bottom of the list, but that doesn't mean you have to wait until all ninety-five receive a heart before you can obtain one. The computer also takes into consideration your urgency code. *High Urgent* is only for acute re-transplantation if the donor heart fails during the actual heart transplant operation, but this is very rare. Your code would no doubt be *Urgent*; it's for those whose condition is deteriorating rapidly and who need a heart in the next few weeks. Other factors come into play that could move you up on the list."

"Like what?" I asked.

"Well, for instance, your blood type is A-Negative, which is not the rarest type, but neither is it among the most common blood groups. So, if an organ of that blood type became available, you would be part of a smaller group of potential recipients. Also, you're a young mother with children at home, and you've had excellent health before you developed heart problems—no obesity, no malignancies or diseases such as diabetes, no tobacco or alcohol use. In addition, you show evidence of emotional and mental stability, and you have a strong support system of family and friends around you. All of those things work in your favor."

I laughed out loud. "I don't know about that emotional stability part. If you only knew what a nervous wreck I've been these last few days just trying to make this decision, you might question whether I had much mental health at all." Dr. Laufer smiled, nodding his understanding.

"Can I ask you a few things about heart transplants?" I asked.

"That's what I'm here for," Dr. Laufer said. "Let's talk."

I had questions prepared that Arland and Dr. Melvin had earlier formulated for me. "First of all, how many transplants do you do in a year at this hospital?"

"Well, so far this year we've done 32 heart transplantations. We're planning on doing 60 by the end of the year. Last year we did 48 and the year before that we did 58."

"And what kind of success rate do you have?"

"If we define success as "survival," then we've had a 90% success rate for the first year."

Arland interjected, "So, you're saying that at the end of one year, 90% of your heart transplant patients are still alive?"

"Yes, that's right. And at the end of five years, 80% of our patients are still alive," Dr. Laufer added.

"How much medical care does the patient need after the transplant?" I asked. "You would be hospitalized for about 30 days. In some cases, the patient is released after 14 days if everything goes extremely well, but that's very rare. In the beginning, you would need weekly biopsies of the heart tissue to see if your body is rejecting it. Several more biopsies would be done during the first year at various intervals. But after that, you would only need a biopsy and a checkup once a year."

My next question was one that Dr. Melvin particularly wanted to know. "If my condition worsens to the point that my other organs also start failing, do you have any mechanical devices to sustain me while we're waiting for a new heart?"

"No, not at this time. Not at our hospital, at least. That's why it's so important that you get on the waiting list for a heart. *Right away.*"

Although I heard the urgency in his voice, I still struggled accepting the fact that my condition was *that* urgent. I continued, "As you probably know, Dr. Laufer, I've been hoping that I could still wait a little longer before deciding to have a transplant. After all, my lungs still seem to function okay as long as they're emptied every few days of the fluid build-up. Can't I continue this way for a while longer?"

"The fact that your lungs are still working is the precise reason a transplant is so critically important *now,*" he said. "This repeated buildup of fluids in your lungs is causing elevated back pressure in the pulmonary arteries. And if this continues much longer, your lungs will suffer permanent damage. When that happens, you will need both a heart *and* a lung transplant. That surgery, of course, is even more difficult and more risky. So, to answer your question— no! You *cannot* continue this way much longer."

Dr. Laufer's emphatic reply startled me, derailing my train of thought for a few moments. While I was struggling to get back on track, Arland spoke up. "Dr. Laufer, you said earlier that you wanted to tell us about the risks involved in a heart transplant."

"Yes, that's the primary thing I want to discuss with you both. Before I get into this, though, you should know that I'm going to paint the bleakest picture possible so that you can fully understand all the risks involved. After an organ transplant, the human body automatically rejects the new organ as a foreign body. You'll need to be put on a drug therapy of cyclosporine and prednisone. These are drugs designed to suppress your immune system so that it won't fight as actively to reject the new heart."

"How long will I have to take these drugs?" I asked.

"Every day for the rest of your life."

I wasn't sure I had heard right. "Do you mean . . . *every* day? . . . *Every single day? . . . Forever?*"

"Yes, every day. Your body will *always* try to reject the new organ as long as you live. Furthermore, you need to be aware of the fact that these drugs may cause physical changes in your body. Things like weight gain, increased hair growth, redness of the skin, facial puffiness, swollen gums, changes in the shape of the face and even malformation of the spine."

"All those things will happen to me just from the effect of the drugs on my body?" I asked.

"No, not all of these things are universally experienced. They're experienced in various measures by different patients. But there's no way of knowing how the drugs will affect *you* until after the transplantation." I sighed deeply several times, agitated by what I had just heard. I shot a nervous look at Arland to express my dismay, but he didn't say anything.

Dr. Laufer continued, "These physical changes are not the only possible effects of the drug therapy, though. There are other more serious side effects that may develop after a few years—conditions such as diabetes, kidney failure, abdominal complications, narrowing of the coronary arteries and hypertension. Also, because your immune system is depressed, you will always have increased risks for infections and cancers. You'll have to be especially careful around large crowds where you could be exposed to respiratory infections. Even childhood diseases like chicken pox and measles could be fatal because your body won't have normal resistance to disease."

As I listened to Dr. Laufer, my eyes welled up with tears. I said, "Your description of life after a heart transplant doesn't sound like any life at all. It's quite alarming, even frightening! Is there anything positive that you can say?"

"As I said, Mrs. Dwelle, that's the worst-case scenario. But it's really a question of the worst versus the worst. Without a different heart, the prospects for your life aren't going to be any better than that. In fact, what you're facing now is potentially much worse than what you'd have to face after a heart transplant."

"Okay, I understand that, but all the same, it still sounds quite depressing." Dr. Laufer again nodded his understanding, pausing to let me absorb the impact of his words. After a few silent moments, I asked, "So, if I sign up today for a transplant, how long will it take before a heart is available?"

"Well, possibly you would have to wait up to nine months, but six months or so would be a normal waiting time for an organ to become available once—"

"Six to nine months?" Arland interjected. "She can't wait that long, can she, Doctor? You just said that her lungs won't function that much longer!"

"Yes, that's true; it *is* a big question whether she can wait that long since her other organs have already started to deteriorate. All we can hope for is that an organ will become available for her sooner than that. But, at the very least, we have to take the first step—signing up for a heart. There's no hope *at all* if she doesn't get on the waiting list for a new heart right away."

Like Arland, I also had a strong reaction to Dr. Laufer's time estimate. But mine was totally different from his. Instead of words of despair, I heard words of hope. *Six to nine months*, I thought to myself, *what a relief! That gives the Lord plenty of time to complete the healing. Yes, plenty of time! I might as well go ahead and sign for the transplant because the Lord's going to heal me long before they ever find a heart for me.*

"Well, Mrs. Dwelle?" Dr. Laufer asked, interrupting my thoughts. "What do you think? Are you willing to be considered as a transplant applicant if a heart becomes available?"

"Yes, I'm ready to sign. In my heart of hearts, I'm not wanting it to happen and I'm hoping it never happens, but I'm willing to become an applicant."

Dr. Laufer nodded with approval and handed me a form. Arland sat beside me as we read through the single sheet written in German. In straightforward language it gave permission to have a heart transplant performed should an organ become available. As I read through the form, a flood of doubts rushed in, filling the reservoir of my emotions. I thought, *This is too strange! Too overwhelming! What am I doing? I'm actually signing my name to exchange my heart for someone else's! I've signed my name thousands of times for insignificant reasons, but this one feels like I'm signing my life away. I can't believe I'm doing this!* I forced myself to hold back the torrent of emotions dammed up inside me.

I penned my signature: **Frances Lois Dwelle.**

While I was still looking over my signed permission form, Arland turned to Dr. Laufer and said, "One more thing we need to ask. How much does it cost to obtain a heart for transplant?"

"There is no charge for the organ itself because an organ cannot be sold or purchased," he said. "It is the free and willing gift of someone who can't keep his or her own life but wishes to extend the life of someone else, someone he or she has never known in most cases. Of course, you will be responsible for costs related to procurement of the organ, costs related to surgery and hospitalization charges."

"I have one more question," I said. "Will you be the doctor who does my heart transplant?"

Dr. Laufer laughed, "Oh, no! We usually leave those surgeries for the younger doctors to do." I didn't say anything, but I thought, *Really? Younger than you?*

Then I handed the signed permission form to Dr. Laufer. "Good," he said. "Next we'll need to take an x-ray to accurately measure the size of the heart for the cavity. Let's plan to do that on Friday, three days from now." He shook my hand and Arland's, and looking us straight in the eyes said, "Mr. and Mrs. Dwelle, I have no doubt that you've made the right decision here today. I wish you the best." With those parting words, he and the three others turned and left the room.

As soon as they were gone, the dam holding back my pent-up emotions broke wide open. I sobbed and sobbed, unable to stop the torrent of tears that flowed. Two nurses ran in and asked what was wrong. "I just can't go through with this! I didn't believe this would ever happen! I can't do it!" They stayed with me for a few minutes, trying to calm me.

After they left, I lay on my bed crying for two more hours. Arland listened as I lamented the loss of any hope for a normal life. "I don't know if I can live that way, Arland. Constant drug therapy. Always at a risk of catching *something*. Until this, I've never had any health problems my whole life. It's too devastating to think of such a catastrophic change in the medical picture of my life."

Arland sat quietly in the chair next to the bed, holding my hand and searching for words to comfort me. After I finally stopped crying, he said, "Fran, you know God has already given us so much grace for this ordeal. Don't you think, if He's led us this far, He's also able to give us the grace and strength to face whatever lies ahead? Why don't we just trust God that if he wants to heal your heart without surgery . . . then fine. If he wants to heal you through a transplant . . . then fine." So, I agreed. That short word of encouragement was what I needed to refocus my thoughts on what had been my strength all along—God's faithful character and His sustaining presence.

Before leaving, Arland prayed, "God, if a heart transplant is your purpose for Fran, please give her the grace to cope with all the changes she'll have to face. If it's possible, would you please reduce the side-effects of the operation and the drugs on Fran's body? And Lord, please help Fran beat all the percentages for a heart transplant patient. Amen."

# Day Eighty-Five (2)

After Arland left, I spent the rest of the night praying, reading my Bible and listening to worship songs on my Walkman. Alone in my private room, I was able to sing and pray aloud without disturbing anyone. Drawing inspiration from the biblical story of the singers who routed the enemy by their praise (2 Chronicles 20), I envisioned the same thing happening in my life. I had always sensed that my health crisis was a battle for my life, so the time had come for me to do battle through prayer and praise. As I sang songs of praise and songs in the Spirit throughout the night, the pall of devastation lifted.

As I finally drifted off to sleep, I prayed, "Thank you, Jesus, for keeping me alive through every crisis. Even if I'm not healed, I will still love and worship you as long as I live. But I ask, Lord, during the six-month wait ahead of me, please complete the healing You've begun . . . so I won't need a transplant."

Just as Arland had experienced a spiritual release in prayer a day earlier, so that night I also encountered God through prayer like I had not done before. After 12 arduous weeks, both of us had at last won our fights against despair, and perhaps—just perhaps—our prayers had also won the battle that would finally bring about the healing of my heart.

Sometime . . . sometime during the middle of that night . . . on June 17, 1992, . . . at Leiden in The Netherlands . . . my name was added to the bottom of the Euro-Transplant waiting list for a donor heart:

*Patient Frances Lois Dwelle; Vienna, Austria*

No one—not me, not Dr. Laufer, not the Euro-Transplant people—had any idea how long it would take for my name to rise to the top of the list. But I had found comfort in Dr. Laufer's hypothetical projection that the waiting period could be as long as six months.

But it was a false comfort. Because that guesstimate was way off. Way . . . Way . . . Off.

# Day Eighty-Six (1)

The day after I signed, the doctors released me for another 48-to-72-hour respite at home. Because of the delay waiting to talk with Dr. Laufer, I had been hospitalized longer than normal that time. As a result, those extra three days of receiving heart stimulants and draining my body of fluids had left me feeling stronger than at any other time since my ordeal began.

Arland picked me up at the hospital at 1:00 p.m., dropped me off at home, and left to run some errands. "I have bills to pay, banking to do, and food to buy," he explained. "I've had no time to do any shopping for weeks now. I need to replenish our groceries in preparation for the long wait ahead of us." I could hear the weariness in his voice. I knew how much he dreaded the thought of standing in Vienna's long grocery lines to buy food.

I was sitting on the couch, half-reading, half-dozing, when the phone rang about 4:00 p.m. Cami answered it and ran back into the room exclaiming, "Mom, it's your doctor. Hurry! Hurry!"

Slowly shuffling to the phone, I thought, *Maybe he's found something out from the most recent batch of tests.* "Hello," I answered. "This is Fran."

"Hello, Mrs. Dwelle. This is Dr. Laufer."

"Yes, Dr. Laufer, what is it?"

His next words stunned me: "Mrs. Dwelle, I'm so excited! We have a heart for you!"

I was too shocked to say anything. Thoughts of disbelief raced through my mind. *What do you mean, 'We have a heart for you?' How can you say this? I must not have heard you right! You told me yesterday it would take at least six months to find a heart. I would never have agreed to something this soon. I can't do this! It's too soon! I'm not emotionally ready for this! Not yet! Not now!*

*NO!*

I felt lightheaded and staggered a step or two backwards, leaning all my weight against the wall."

"Mrs. Dwelle?"

"Yes, I'm still here," I responded weakly. "Are you sure this is right, Dr. Laufer?"

*"Are you sure?"*

"Yes, it's perfect for you. It's the right size and blood type." Dr. Laufer, who was normally calm and reserved, was so excited. He repeated, "It's perfect, Mrs. Dwelle! We've already sent Dr. Simon to Germany to bring back the heart. You need to be here at the *AKH*, the Vienna General Hospital, in two hours. Come to room D200 in the Cardiac Care Unit. That's in two hours, Mrs. Dwelle. It's very important that you be here at the *AKH* no later than six o'clock."

My thoughts were racing out of control: *How could they send someone to get a heart without calling me first? Why did they assume that I would automatically consent to go ahead with the operation? Just because I agreed to go on the waiting list? Am I supposed to be happy that I moved up above ninety-five others to the top of the list? Well, maybe I should be happy about all that . . . but I'm not!*

"Mrs. Dwelle?"

"Yes, Dr. Laufer. No! I mean no, I'm not sure I'm ready for this. I can't believe this has happened so quickly. And besides, my husband's not home right now, and he would want to know about this." Cami was by the phone, listening to every word. With a wide-eyed look, she spread her hands out, palms up, shrugging her shoulders as if to ask, *What's going on?* I mouthed a silent scream to her.

"Yes, it *is* sudden," he continued. "I understand how you feel. But sometimes these things happen very quickly. All you have to do is be at the *AKH* by 6:00 p.m., okay?"

"Okay, thank you, Dr. Laufer." And I hung up. That was it. The entire conversation was curt, very straight forward, lasting no more than two minutes. Dr. Laufer never asked me if I wanted to go through with the operation. He just assumed that I would be there in two hours.

As soon as I hung up, I collapsed into a chair and burst into tears. "They have a heart for me, Cami! They have a heart for me!" I wailed. "How can this be possible, Cami? How can they do a heart transplant on me so soon?"

I cried some more and soon we were both wailing. Between sobs, I repeated, "I can't believe this is happening . . . I can't do this . . . *I just can't do this!* . . . I have to let someone know about this . . . I can't go through this by myself . . . Where is Arland? . . . Where's Daddy? . . . Where is he? . . . Why isn't he here?"

After a few minutes, I dried my tears, took some deep breaths, and decided to phone some friends. *I don't have to be alone in this,* I thought. *I can get some people praying for me.* So, I called our Vienna missions office to talk to Bobby and Sheryl Beard. They were out of the country, but I talked to the secretary. "I just found out I'm going in for a heart transplant," I told her. "I can't believe it. I really don't think I can go through this. Please call everybody and have them pray," I sobbed.

The office secretary called a number of people in the city, including Bobi and Nancy Arsenovich, missionary colleagues living in Vienna. Then I left a message for the Beards and another one for Greg and Sandie in the States.

The first person to call me was Pastor Danny. I repeated the same things. "Danny, they have a heart for me! I can't believe this is happening to me. I can't go through this. I had expected all along that God was going to heal my heart. I don't understand why this is happening. Arland's not even here. I don't know where he is. I have no idea how I'm going to get to the hospital."

"Fran, don't worry about it," Danny said. "We'll get somebody over there to take you to the hospital, and I'll call Dr. Melvin right away."

Danny hung up and five minutes later Dr. Melvin called. "Fran, I heard what happened. What exactly did they tell you? Do you know where you're supposed to go?"

"The only thing Dr. Laufer said was that they had a heart for me and that I needed to be at the *AKH* by 6:00 p.m. I need to go to the Cardiac Care Unit, but I haven't the faintest idea where this is. All my treatment has been done at the *Wilhelminenspital*, so I don't know where anything is at the *AKH*. It's such a large complex. And I don't know where Arland is either."

"Well, Fran, time is of the essence," Dr. Melvin said. "Okay, tell you what. The place you need to go to is close to my office. I'll go over there right now and find out where you need to report. You'll need to leave your home no later than 5:30 if you're going to get to the hospital by 6:00. I'll call your friend Mary Ginter and see if she can drive you in case Arland doesn't return in time. So, Fran, don't worry about anything. I'll see to it that you make it to the hospital on time."

Fifteen minutes later, Dr. Melvin called back. "Yes, Fran, I went over there and found out where the station is that you're to go to. They already know about you and they're expecting you. I'll give Mary that information, but we'll keep waiting for Arland to come home. I'll call you back periodically to see if he's returned. So, don't worry, Fran—everything's under control."

I felt a little bit more confident. Just a little bit. My emotions were still bouncing, my thoughts were still whirling, and the pit in my stomach was still cavernous. But I was relieved that Dr. Melvin would take care of getting me to the hospital. *He's a godsend, Lord,* I said to myself. During every conversation, Cami was glued next to me the whole time, listening and absorbing every detail.

By then it was 4:35, and I had less than an hour left to pack a suitcase. At that moment, Jessi arrived home from school. When Cami saw her coming, she ran outside, yelling from the top of the steps, "Jessi, hurry up! Mom's getting ready to go to the hospital. She's going to have a heart transplant!" Jessi ran up the stairs and into the house, her eyes wide and her mouth agape. She just stood there speechless.

From that point on the phone rang incessantly. Nancy called and offered to bring supper and stay with the kids. I accepted the offer and thanked her. Greg phoned from the States a few seconds later. I could hear in his voice that he was fighting back tears. I asked him, "Greg, do you think it would be okay if I just refused the heart and asked to be kept on the waiting list for a heart at a later date? I'm not emotionally ready for this. Besides, that would give the Lord more time to complete the healing."

"Fran, I don't think you can do that. In the Austrian culture, it's an offense to them if you refuse their favors. And you might never get another chance like this. My advice is that you have to take *this* particular heart. I understand how traumatic this is for you, but you *have* to do it, Fran. *Now!*" After Greg prayed for me over the phone, I felt less fearful. Although the idea of a transplant was still difficult to accept, I was beginning to resign myself to the inevitability of one.

Greg hung up and immediately Ginger called. "Fran, we're all behind you," she said. "I'm calling everyone I know in the city to have them pray for you. You're going to make it through this!" Knowing Ginger, I had no doubt that she would have an army of prayer support organized before the day was over.

Ginger hung up and Dr. Melvin called back. "Is Arland home yet? Do you know where he could be? Is there any way we can try to trace him down?"

"He went shopping today, and I have no clue where he's at," I answered. "Besides, I'm concerned for *him* right now. I don't know how much more of this stress *he* can take. He's already completely exhausted, and I don't see how he can handle another crisis like this one." Dr. Melvin said he would check back in another fifteen minutes.

As soon as he hung up, I got a call from Bob Schmidgall, our long-time pastor friend from the States. I expressed my surprise: "Bob, how did you find out about my situation?"

"Greg called the headquarters office and they contacted me. How are you feeling about everything, Fran?"

"I'm in a daze, Bob. I can't believe this is happening. It's way too quick. I don't think that I can go through with it." I started to cry again. "I've been expecting God to heal my heart, and here I am going in for transplant surgery. I never thought it would come to this."

"Well, Fran, it could end up being similar to what happened to Abraham," Bob said. "Even while he was on the way to make the sacrifice, he was expecting God to do a miracle. And God *did* do it at the last moment. If God wanted to, He could wait until the knife is in the surgeon's hand to complete your healing. Fran, I think you need to proceed with preparation for the surgery and leave the outcome to God." Then he prayed that the Lord would heal my heart, asking God to give me peace to trust Him if I were to have a heart transplant.

After he hung up, several other friends called. They all got the same litany, and in every conversation I cried. I felt like an emotional wreck, totally out of control, unlike I had ever been before.

Dr. Melvin called again. "No," I said. "No Arland. No word from him. No idea where he's at."

In the meantime, our mission office in the States phoned our families to inform them of the surgery. But no family member was able to get through to me on the phone. At 5:00, Mary Ginter arrived to drive me to the hospital in case Arland didn't make it home by 5:30. A few minutes later, Bobi and Nancy arrived to stay with the girls.

At 5:05, Dr. Melvin called again. "No . . . Nothing . . . No, I don't know."

After that, the phone stopped ringing. I was trying to get my things together. Everyone in the room was quietly somber. I was weepy—not sobbing, but my eyes constantly brimming with tears. Cami was crying softly. Jessi was stone silent. As the two girls helped me pack, my thoughts turned to Kaci at college back in the States. *I wonder who's going to contact her? Lord, please help someone remember to do that.* I was too wrung out to make any more calls.

In the midst of this turmoil, two Scriptures kept coming to my mind. The first was Psalm 46, verse 1: "God is our refuge and strength; an ever-present help in time of trouble." *A present help,* I thought. *Lord, You will help me presently in whatever I need. And if ever I've needed Your help, Lord, it's now!*

I also recalled the promise in Proverbs 18, verse 10: "The name of the Lord is a strong tower; the righteous run to it and are safe." For a brief moment, I pondered the possibility that I might not come out of the surgery alive. In my spirit I prayed, *Lord, this is the most unbearable thing I have ever faced in my life. You alone are my hope, my strength, and my place of safety. But if I'm not going to live through the surgery, then I'm ready.*

It was 5:20. No one had called for fifteen minutes.

The phone rang. "No, Dr. Melvin . . . No Arland . . . Nothing."

After hanging up, my eyes welled up with tears again at the thought of not having Arland with me. *How could he not be with me now? After all we've been through together the past three months, how could he not be here with me for this, the most traumatic hour of my life?*

It was 5:25. I was sitting on the couch ready to go, my two small bags on the floor by the door. Jessi was sitting close to me. Cami was by the front window, her eyes glued to the street below. Bobi and Nancy were sitting across the room. Mary was leaning against the piano, unaware that she was jingling the keys in her hand. No one could think of anything to say. We were just waiting, waiting for Dr. Melvin to call one last time. Then I would have to leave for the hospital.

Suddenly, Cami jumped up from her perch by the window. "It's Daddy!" she gasped as she bolted toward the door. "Daddy's home!"

It was 5:30.

# Day Eighty-Six (2)

'No, Cami! Don't tell him," Jessi cried out. "Let Mom tell him. Wait 'till he gets up here."

But Cami ignored her sister, rushed outside, and raced down the steps to the iron gate. She yelled across the street to Arland as he got out of the car, "Daddy, hurry up! You've got to come up here right now! *Right now, Dad!* Mom has to go to the hospital to get a new heart. *Right now!*"

"What? What did you say?"

"*Right now,* Dad. She has to leave *right now.*"

Arland bounded up the walkway steps, two at a time, and burst into the house. "Fran, what's happening," he blurted out. "Fran, tell me. *What is going on?*" Before I could answer he turned to the girls and said, "Quick, Jessi, you and Cami go get the groceries."

"I don't think I can do this, Arland. I have to be at the hospital in thirty minutes. They have a heart for me. *They already have a heart for me!*" I sobbed. "I can't go through this. I'm just not ready for this. Not now. Maybe later, but not now!"

Arland came over to the couch and sat beside me. Taking my hand, he said, "Fran, this is it! You have to take *this* heart. You have no other choice. This is what we've been waiting for. You *can* do it. You *will* make it just fine. You're stronger now than you've been in weeks, so it's no coincidence that the Lord made a heart available *today* to you. You *can* do it. *Today!* The Lord will help you through it. We'll all be here for you."

Just then the phone rang. "You answer it, Arland. I'm sure it's Dr. Melvin."

"Thank God you're home, Arland," Dr. Melvin exclaimed. "Quick, time is of the essence! Let me tell you how to get to the hospital's cardiac care building." Arland listened, restating the directions back to Dr. Melvin: "Turn left on . . . then go straight on . . . turn again onto . . ." Several times he stopped Dr. Melvin and asked him to repeat himself.

Finally, Dr. Melvin said, "I know a simpler way to do this. I'll just take you directly there. If I leave now, I can make it to the corner of *Dornbacher Strasse* and *Alser Strasse* before you get there. It's a major intersection not too far from the hospital. There's a busy tram stop there, and I'll be standing in the center median strip. I'll flag you down when I see you coming, so look for me. Then I'll take you directly to the hospital."

Arland thanked him and hung up. He then took the girls and me into the adjoining study for a few private moments. He prayed a simple prayer: "Father, give Fran your strength and your peace. Give the doctors wisdom. Please make this operation a complete success. Thank you for your goodness to us all. You have never failed us once, and we love you and trust you with our lives."

As I whispered a quiet "Amen," I added a silent prayer: *And Lord, please help someone reach Kaci wherever she's at right now.* I held both of my daughters for a few moments, kissing them several times. Cami cried profusely, clinging to me. Jessi hugged me tightly and silently, too distraught to say anything. Then we came back into the living room, and I hugged my other friends. There were no words, just more tears.

As we walked out the door, Bobi said, "If it's all right, Arland, I'd like to go to the hospital and just be there with you."

Arland immediately answered, "Sure, Bobi, by all means we'd love to have you come with us." I was pleased because I knew Bobi's strong, quiet presence would provide support for Arland during the long hours of my surgery. *Especially if the worst happened,* I thought.

As I slowly walked to the car, down one step after another, I recited the same two Scriptures over and over in my mind: *The Lord is an ever-present help . . . a present help; The name of the Lord is a strong tower . . . I can run to Him and be safe.* At that crisis hour in my life, nothing but my confidence in God's character could stabilize the emotional upheaval I was experiencing.

By the time we left, we were already ten minutes behind schedule for the trip to the hospital. In the first part of the drive, no one said a word. Then I broke the silence by vocalizing my obsession again. "I really expected God to heal my heart, Arland. What if He does heal it and they don't know? What if they take out my *healed* heart?" Arland did not respond, so I babbled the same concerns again, as much to myself as to him. Still no response.

Arland was preoccupied with his own obsession—time. "Fran, we have to get you there to check in by six o'clock. Dr. Melvin said the timing is critical. All of your prep has to be done so you're in the operating room with your body cooled down by the time the heart reaches the hospital. He said there could not be *any* delays. If you're not ready, then the heart deteriorates. He said even five or ten minutes can make a difference." Arland grumbled on about the heavy traffic and the long lights and how this was the worst time of the day to be driving.

While we were going through the streets of Vienna, I thought to myself, *Look at all this—everywhere else life is going on as normal. But my life is so abnormal! Here I am, going to the hospital for a heart transplant, but no one out there is even aware of it. They're preoccupied with window-shopping, buying bakery, sipping coffee, waiting for trams, reading papers, and walking dogs. How could they all be so oblivious to the fact that today my life is going to be changed f-o-r-e-v-e-r?*

As we approached the intersection of *Dornbacher Strasse* and *Alser Strasse*, Dr. Melvin saw us coming. Still wearing his white hospital jacket, he had run a half-mile to station himself on the center-island tram stop. For 15 minutes he had been looking intently at every car passing by. When he spotted our car, he began waving his arms frantically. Arland and I both started laughing at the sight of this 6-foot, 200-pound doctor, jumping up and down in the middle of a busy four-lane street. As we slowed down, Dr. Melvin hopped into the back seat, not waiting for the car to come to a complete stop. He must have immediately sensed our anxiety because—without even saying hello—he calmly said, "Don't worry; we'll make it."

Arland was planning to turn left at that corner, and then take a straight shot to the hospital. But no left turn was permitted. Dr. Melvin gasped, "Oh, no! I didn't realize you couldn't turn here! I never drive to the hospital; I always take the tram."

So Arland turned right, in the opposite direction of the hospital. He tried backtracking but ended up on a narrow winding street only wide enough for one car. He turned onto another one-way street, but it was blocked off by construction. Turning around, he started down another street that ended abruptly. We were stuck in a maze of one-way and dead-end streets.

While Arland looked for a way to escape this labyrinth, I got on my favorite subject again. "Dr. Melvin," I said, "you've done a lot of transplants, right? Do they do any last-minute checks on the heart to determine its condition?"

"Well, yes, they make one last examination of the heart and your other vital organs before they start the transplant procedure."

"Good, because I'm still praying for God to heal my heart, and I don't want them to take out my healed heart. Is that okay?"

Dr. Melvin looked at me quizzically and muttered, "Yes, um . . . well, yea okay." He didn't voice anything else, but the look on his face said, *I can't believe you're saying this. You're asking me, of all people, that question? After all, I'm a heart transplant surgeon. What do you expect me to think? Why can't you just accept this operation as God's answer to your prayers?* But I could not let go of the hope that God was still going to heal my heart.

When I realized that neither Arland nor Dr. Melvin knew how to get to the hospital, I became panicky. I could feel the pressure building for the six o'clock countdown. Dr. Melvin was quite calm, outwardly, but he kept looking at his watch every thirty seconds. All of a sudden, he recognized a familiar street. "Quick, Arland, we've got no choice now. Time is of the essence. Make a wrong-way turn onto this next street." Arland never questioned him. After checking the traffic, he made an illegal turn onto the next street. One block later he turned onto the street that took us directly to the hospital.

At exactly 6:00 p.m., we pulled up to the *AKH* entrance and squealed to a halt at the guard station. Dr. Melvin showed the guard his credentials, and we were waved through. Arland gunned the car and we screeched into the hospital grounds. Driving through a big green metal gate and past a number of buildings, we finally came to the cardiac care building. Cars were double-parked everywhere. Dr. Melvin said, "Park in the restricted lot for physicians, Arland. We have an emergency here, so we don't have time to drive around looking for a parking spot."

I kidded him as we got out of the car. "Dr. Melvin, you're my angel in white today. What a godsend you've been! We could have never found this place by ourselves. You didn't have to do all this, but thank you so much."

"Fran, it's my pleasure to do this for you. It's at least one small way that I can help you with all that you're facing today."

I slowly shuffled toward the hospital building, leaning all my weight on Arland. Double glass doors welcomed us into a dimly lit foyer. No one was in the entrance area and no wheelchair was anywhere in sight. The gray floor tiles amplified our arrival, step by step. As Dr. Melvin led us down the hallway, I reiterated for the umpteenth time, "I can't believe this is really happening to me. I just can't believe I'm having a heart transplant." No one responded to my mutterings. Even the institutional-green walls ignored my sighs, bouncing every word back.

An ancient creaky elevator took us up several floors. Arland, Bobi and Dr. Melvin chitchatted about the elevator's primitive technology. I was silent. Dr. Melvin pushed the buttons and the elevator deposited us at the appropriate floor.

It was 6:10 p.m. when the four of us walked into the hospital ward. Dr. Melvin helped me check in at the registration window, and then he and Bobi left for the waiting room. When I told the receptionist my name, she said, "Yes, we are expecting you, Frances Dwelle. It says here that you don't have any insurance coverage. Is that right?"

"Well, I have insurance which has covered the hospitalizations for my heart problems. But, no, it doesn't cover the costs for a transplantation," I said in German. I understood, of course, that meant I would now receive the lowest class of treatment, Class C, not the first-class care I had been given previously.

After the brief registration process was completed, they led Arland and me to my assigned ward, not to a private room like I had been in previously. When we walked in, I was startled to see how stark the room was. Three women patients and three empty beds filled the large dingy room. None of the women spoke to me or even acknowledged my presence. They occupied the three corner beds, so I took the other corner bed right next to a sink. That left an empty middle bed on each side of the room.

The nurse gave me the by-now-all-too-familiar-pale-yellow hospital gown. I was too weak to undress myself so Arland helped me. When the other women heard Arland and me speaking in English, they watched with rapt curiosity. I had absolutely no privacy. For a few minutes I was the center of attention in that room. Arland helped me undress and then put away my clothes, meticulously straightening them on the hangars and positioning my shoes on the floor with the heels evenly matched. We sat together on the bed in silence for a few minutes. I felt very strange, still finding it hard to believe that I was going in for a heart transplant. During this entire time, none of the women said a word. They just gawked at me as if I were a sideshow.

Five minutes later the nurse came, took me out for blood work, and sent Arland to the waiting room. They drew several vials of blood, and then they sent me down for x-rays. I waited almost thirty minutes to get into the x-ray room. I thought to myself, *What a waste of time! We had to rush like crazy to get here because time was supposed to be so critical, and now we're wasting all this time.* During this waiting period, I was able to relax a little. I prayed silently the whole time, thanking God that He was in control and praising Him for His goodness.

When I returned to my room, Arland came back and sat beside me. "Well, Arland, here we are," I said. "Can you believe that it's all come down to this? Well, I still can't. I'm still praying for God to heal my heart, so I won't have to go through this surgery. I hope the doctors remember to check my heart once more before they do the transplant."

Right until the last hour, I clung to my hope that God was going to complete the healing of my heart. *After all,* I reasoned, *why else would Jesus have visited me if it were not to heal my heart? I would have died within a few days had He not touched me that night in my hospital room. Surely, the only reason He kept me alive for all these weeks was because He intended to finish the healing He began.*

Danny came and encouraged Arland and me. He held our hands and prayed that God would complete my healing through this transplant. I still could not understand how a transplant represented a "healing," but I finally was willing to accept whatever God chose. We kept our voices just above a whisper, adding to the intrigue of this whole scene for the other three women patients.

I was amazed that I felt no fear at all. Just incredible peace. Even though I was still hoping the transplant wouldn't happen, I trusted that God would do what was best. No one mentioned the possibility that I might not survive the operation, but it was certainly on my mind.

After another wait, two attendants finally came at 8:15 with a stretcher-bed. As soon as they lifted me onto the bed, I started crying. I had the same recurring thought: *Lord, I still believe you can heal my heart. If you choose not to, then I still trust You to get me through this operation.*

When they pushed my bed into the hall, everyone who had been waiting outside rushed to gather around me. They hovered over me as I was lying flat on my back. Danny, Bobi, Dr. Melvin, and several others all squeezed my hand and told me they would be praying. Some of them had tears streaming down their faces.

Arland leaned over me. He was somber but calm. His blue eyes gazed tenderly at me for a few moments. Then he kissed me, whispering in my ear, "Good-bye, Fran. I love you."

I pressed my moist cheek against his. "I love you too, Honey," was all I said. No other words came to mind. Besides, there was no more time for words—my bed had already started moving away.

Tears coursed down my cheeks as the gurney carried me quickly down the hall. I tried to look up, but the harsh white ceiling panels blinded me. Again, I affirmed the truth of Psalm 46:1 in my heart: *The Lord is my refuge and strength, an ever-present, an ever-present help in trouble. Therefore, I will not fear.* I prayed, "Lord, You can still heal me if that's Your will. But I submit to you. I am at peace with whatever You want." I felt no fear.

A cranky service elevator took my bed down two floors. The male nurse chatted in German to me, but I was totally disinterested. He parked the bed in a little alcove outside the operating room and left me. The waiting area was frigid, and the thin sheet offered little protection from the cold. As I shivered, I thought of Arland and my friends upstairs. Tears flowed again. I thought of my girls and my family. More tears flowed. I lay there for ten more minutes, shaking and freezing.

Soon a different male nurse came out to prep me for surgery. He shaved me with a dry razor. It bothered me that the hospital didn't have a female nurse do this for a woman, but I was too weary to voice an objection.

I felt so alone.

At 8:30, my bed was wheeled through the double doors into the operating room. It was even colder there than in the hallway. A doctor started to speak to me in German. I didn't have enough mental energy left to process German, so I told him I didn't understand. Another doctor spoke up, "She's an American; she only speaks English."

"How do you feel?" he asked in English.

"I feel fine, but I'm very cold."

"Do you have any pain?"

"No, I'm just very cold."

I was lifted onto the operating table and covered up. I responded weakly again, "I'm so cold." Someone brought me another blanket.

I had never been hospitalized at the *AKH*, so I knew none of the five doctors. But they all seemed to understand how traumatized I felt. The two women doctors especially tried to relieve my anxiety by smiling warmly, speaking kindly and touching me gently.

One of them explained to me what would happen. "The anesthesiologist will come soon. He will prepare you for the operation by putting you to sleep. He'll start the intravenous anesthetic and give you an injection. Your speech will become slurred. Then you will become very sleepy. The next thing you'll know will be when you wake up. It will be all over. Any questions?"

I thought, *Any questions? You have no idea how many questions I have! But I don't think you really want to hear them. Besides, I don't think you or anyone else can answer my questions.* I shook my head *no* and asked, "Where's Dr. Laufer? I don't see him in here."

"He'll be here soon," she replied. "Dr. Laufer told you, didn't he, that he will be the one supervising the surgery, not the one performing it?" I nodded, *yes.* She continued, "The surgeon who will perform the surgery is Dr. Simon. He's on his way here."

A few minutes later the anesthesiologist arrived. He and the other doctors talked to me while prepping me for surgery. Not once were the words *heart* or *heart transplant* mentioned by any of them. I never initiated any conversations either. I was silent, still in shock, trying to comprehend the weightiness of all that had happened in just five hours. Over and over, I heard Dr. Laufer's words replaying in my mind—*we have a heart for you.* And every time the message replayed itself, my emotions screamed out all over again, *No! How can this be? No! I'm not ready!*

I started to feel drowsy. I wanted to stay awake long enough to meet Dr. Simon, the surgeon who would remove my heart, but he still had not arrived.

As I lay under the bright lights, listening to the beeping heart monitor, I prayed again, *Only You, Lord, can still heal my heart. And if You choose to do so, please help the doctors NOT take out my healed heart! For You alone are my strength; You alone are my refuge; You alone are my tower of safety; You alone are my ever-present help.*

I became drowsier, unable to keep my eyes open. As I was slipping away, I heard a phone ring somewhere in the distance. I heard a woman doctor report in German to the others, "Dr. Simon's plane has just landed."

I turned my last thoughts to my God. *And Lord . . . if I don't . . . wake up . . . well then . . . I know . . . for . . . sure . . . that . . . I'll . . . be . . . with . . . You . . . for . . . You . . . a . . . lone . . . are . . . my . . . pres . . . ent . . . .*

# Day Eighty-Six (3)

When Dr. Simon laid eyes on me for the first time, I was already unconscious. He had planned it that way. The anesthetic had knocked me out at the precise time called for in the heart transplantation protocol. During the previous five hours—while I had been fussing and fuming, weeping and wailing, pleading and praying—Dr. Simon had been working feverishly to procure a heart for me.

A telephone call earlier that day had signaled the beginning of Dr. Simon's six-hour odyssey to procure this heart. The Euro-Transplant computer in Leiden, The Netherlands, decided at 3:15 p.m. on June 17, 1992, that *"patient Frances Dwelle living in Vienna, Austria,"* was the best candidate for an organ that had just become available. The Leiden coordinator called the Intensive Care Unit at the *AKH* in Vienna. Immediately, ICU paged Dr. Andreas Zuckerman, the transplant coordinator for the *AKH*, who was working a normal busy day doing biopsies at the outpatient clinic. "There's a possible organ donor from Leiden," the nurse told him. "Come right over and get the information."

He rushed to the ICU to evaluate the data. First, he double-checked my records. Then he called Leiden back to verify routine information about the donor—age, weight, height, and blood group. He asked if any special drugs had been given to hold the arterial pressure of the patient. He decided that everything looked fine. I was ready for the transplant and there was a good donor.

Next, Dr. Zuckerman needed to find a place for me in ICU. Because of a shortage of nurses, all the allotted beds were full. He contacted the anesthesiologist on duty who decided to transfer one patient out of ICU to an intermediate care unit. After securing a bed for me, he called Professor Wollner, the head of the cardiac-thoracic department at the *AKH.* "We have an organ offer and we want to transplant Mrs. Dwelle. Do you remember her?" he asked. "She's the patient at the *Wilhelminenspital* with the unusual blood problem."

"Yes, I know about her, and I know that her situation is urgent," Dr. Wollner replied. "Okay, do it! Go for it!" In twenty minutes, Dr. Zuckerman had verified the transplant data, received clearance from capacity control, and secured the approval of his superior.

Next, he found out from the procurement hospital in Germany the exact time that the organ ex-plantation had to be done. *Everything else* would be scheduled in reference to this critical piece of information. He then communicated those findings to Dr. Simon, the doctor who would remove the heart from the donor and perform the transplant surgery on me. (The Vienna transplant doctors did not allow any other doctor team in Europe to harvest the heart.) Then he called the *Wilhelminenspital* to arrange my transfer by ambulance to the *AKH* by 6:00 p.m. When he heard that I had been discharged a few hours earlier, he asked Dr. Laufer to contact me at home.

After that, he telephoned *Errtevolk Ambulanz,* which had a pilot ready twenty-four hours a day for emergencies. He contracted a medical flight to Germany and alerted his hospital to ready a vehicle for an airport run. Finally, he called the operating room with the timing details for the transplantation and asked them to prepare the necessary procurement items: an ice chest filled with crushed ice used for storing the heart, bottles of profusion solution for cooling down the heart, cross-clamps and other specialized instruments used for harvesting an organ.

At 4:00 p.m., when I received the fateful *we-have-a-heart-for-you* call at home, Doctors Simon and Zuckerman were already racing to the Vienna airport in an emergency vehicle, horns blaring and blue lights flashing. Thirty minutes later, their medical emergency plane was airborne, hastened by Air Traffic Control's suspension of all other landings and takeoffs. Ninety minutes later, they landed in Germany, hurried into a waiting ambulance, and arrived at the procurement hospital by 6:30 p.m.

Meanwhile, I was completing my check-in procedures at the *AKH* in Vienna at the same time the doctors started their procurement procedure in Germany. Dr. Simon examined the donor heart which had been kept vital following her demise. After determining everything was okay, Dr. Zuckerman phoned back to the ICU in Vienna and told them to start preparing me for the operation.

Dr. Simon then used a special solution to cool the heart down to four degrees Celsius, causing cardiac arrest in the female donor. Then he clamped the aorta, a procedure that signaled the start of the ischemic time frame for the transplantation. Within four hours of that aorta cross clamp, the donor heart had to be sewn into my chest and fully pumping. From the point of the clamping onward, everything had to be scheduled right to the minute. Right down to the minute!

The actual organ procurement went quickly. In less than ten minutes, Dr. Simon had removed the heart with surgical scissors. After examining it further, he wrapped the heart in towels to protect it from freezing and put it into a plastic bag filled with ice-cold solution. He removed all air from the bag before closing it. Next, he put that bag into another bag filled with profusion solution and then into a third bag of the same liquid. Then he put this big three-in-one bag, with the heart safe in the innermost sac, into a cooler filled with crushed ice.

After quickly changing from their O.R. greens back into white coats, the two doctors ran—literally—to a waiting ambulance, toting the picnic-sized cooler between them. They had harvested the heart in thirty minutes.

At 7:30 p.m., they arrived back at the German airport for their ninety-minute return flight to Vienna. As their Learjet neared Vienna, all air traffic was stacked up in order to give their plane priority. The jet landed and the two doctors hurried inside to the customs counter. After running the ice chest through the security screen, they grabbed their precious cargo and raced past the immigration counter. The immigration official tried to stop them, yelling, "Wait! Where's your passports? Wait, you can't—"

"We're the transplant team! We don't need passports!" Dr. Zuckerman yelled back at him. The official weakly objected, but it was too late; they were already heading out the terminal exit doors.

Once outside, an ambulance was waiting to take them on the last fifteen-minute leg of their trip. As the van accelerated away, Dr. Zuckerman made one more call to the O.R. transplant team. "We're on the way!" he exclaimed to Dr. Laufer.

That call meant one thing: *the time had come.* The time to remove my heart had finally come. There was no time left to wait for a miracle—not another day, not another hour.

While the heart-with-my-name-on-it was speeding in an ambulance to the *AKH,* the surgical team started the removal process. By then I was already out, having fully yielded my body to the power of the anesthetic and to the will of my Lord.

The first incision was made, and my thorax was cut open. Then my heart was put on bypass—not removed yet, just put on bypass—and made ready for immediate removal as soon as the new heart arrived. If for some reason the transplant would not be possible, *or necessary,* the doctors would still have the option to wean me off bypass and back to the full use of my old heart.

At 9:30 p.m., the journey to procure a heart for me—*patient Frances Lois Dwelle of Vienna, Austria*—came to an end. With the ice chest firmly in grasp, Dr. Zuckerman marched into the operating room. "Good luck!" was all he said as he handed it to one of the surgeons. And just as quickly as he entered, he turned around and left, striding out briskly with an air of accomplishment.

Meanwhile, Dr. Simon quickly changed into his O.R. greens and prepared for surgery. Dr. Laufer and his team had already reconfirmed that my heart was irreparably damaged. So, Dr. Simon did not need to do another examination before continuing with the surgery.

Everything was set. Nothing now could stop the transplant from proceeding.

My 44-year-old heart had passed the medical point of no return.

# Day Eighty-Six (4)

Arland regarded this *night of no return* as a providential act far more than anyone else could appreciate, including me. Day and night, he had been on a quest to determine what caused my heart problems and how to resolve those problems. But the sudden provision of a donor heart had abruptly changed everything. It meant that the long-sought-for answers were finally ... possibly ... hopefully ... coming into view.

In the surgery waiting room, Arland welcomed the company of the others with him: Dr. Melvin, Bobi, Danny, and my friends, Angela, Wolfgang, and Carolyn. But after a while, Arland struggled to control his anxieties about my operation. To occupy his mind, he engaged Dr. Melvin with question after question about the procedures involved in heart transplantation. Dr. Melvin understood Arland's makeup well. He knew that by satisfying Arland's thirst for information, he would also be calming his frayed nerves. So, he walked him through each step of the operation saying, "About now, Arland, they're doing this. Next, they'll start this procedure. After that—" His simple explanations removed the mystique surrounding a heart transplant, making it appear as if a heart transplant was an accepted, normal procedure. Of course, to Dr. Melvin it was; after all, he had done more than 100 heart transplants himself.

"From a technical aspect," he explained, "a heart transplant is a simpler procedure than bypass surgery. You don't have to fool around with all the tiny blood vessels. But instead, you're taking the heart out as a whole and replacing it. The only sutures required are on the larger vessels and on the heart muscle itself. From the standpoint of the dexterity required in a surgeon, it's much easier to do a heart transplant than to do repair or splicing of smaller blood vessels."

He also detailed the possible problems associated with transplantation and, particularly, the kind of life a patient would face following this surgery. But he concluded, "I have no doubt this transplant will be successful. You can be sure of one thing, Arland—Fran's life will be immeasurably improved over what it's been." After giving an hour-long mini seminar, he left the hospital, explaining that he had a lot to do before moving back to the States in a few days. As always, Dr. Melvin was optimistic, and his early departure conveyed the same positive message: *I'm sure everything's going to be just fine—there's no need for me to stick around.*

Two hours into my surgery, Arland began pacing back and forth in the waiting room. Eventually, he left the others to go find a public phone. He made his first attempt to call Kaci in the States but could not reach her. Then he decided to look for a place where he could get alone with his thoughts. At the bottom of two flights of stairs, he found a remote alcove that he turned into a makeshift chapel. There he poured out his heart to God, imploring Him to bring me safely through the surgery. Several more times that night, he left the waiting room to revisit this private sanctuary, and each time he found solace there for his anxious soul.

As the wait neared four hours, Arland went outside and began walking the grounds, staying in areas that were lit by gas lanterns. He decided to see if he could find out where my surgery was happening. As he circled the grounds of the medical complex, he noticed that the whole third floor on one side of the building was lit up. He thought, *Nothing else would be going on at this time of night except Fran's surgery. That must be where Fran's at.* But from the ground level, he could not see into the windows located on the upper floor.

Then he noticed a long set of outdoor stairs going up the side of a building adjoining the cardiac center. Running over there, he charged up the steps until he reached a landing near the top. There he found himself at eye-level with the windows on the surgery floor. From this vantage point only thirty feet away, he could see into the surgical theatre. The operating tables were out of view, but he could plainly see Dr. Laufer standing by one of the windows, looking at several monitoring screens. Arland thought, *The only monitors that would interest Dr. Laufer at this time of night have to be related to Fran's surgery.* Exhilarated that he had found my operating location, he rejoiced with thanks to God for this small provision.

Arland transfixed his gaze on that third-floor window, oblivious to anything else going on in the building. Dr. Laufer would reappear every time he had to check the monitoring screens, and then he would disappear again after he got his data. Sometimes, he glanced at his monitors for a few brief moments; other times, he lingered in front of the screens for several minutes. This recurring scene captivated Arland's total attention for almost an hour as he stood there motionless in the warm evening air.

While he was observing this drama, spellbound by Dr. Laufer's sporadic appearances in the window of the surgical theater, Arland occupied the time in prayer. *Please, Lord, make the operation successful,* he pleaded. *Give wisdom to Dr. Laufer. Guide the hands of Dr. Simon and his surgical team. Accomplish Your perfect will. And . . . please, Lord, . . . spare Fran's life.* He prayed these requests again . . . and again. That stairway was his personal prayer platform, a sacred altar—so to speak—for seeking God's grace.

About 1:30 a.m., Dr. Laufer again came over to the monitors, but this time he turned them off, one by one. Arland's pulse quickened as he watched Dr. Laufer disappear from view. A few moments later, all the overhead lights went out and the entire third floor went black. Arland froze on the spot, his heart pounding in his chest. He thought to himself, *Oh Lord, what has just happened? Is it all over now? Wasn't the surgery supposed to take longer than this? Does this mean they've finished the operation and Fran has a new heart? Or, does this mean she didn't make it? Dear Lord, what's going on?*

For several more minutes, he just stood there, motionless, searching the darkness for an explanation. His unanswered question—*Is Fran alive or dead*—felt like a crushing weight on his chest, making it hard to breathe. He knew one thing for sure—it was over. One way or another, *it was all over!*

While staring blankly at the darkened windows, suddenly he noticed movement below. A door on the ground floor of the building opened, and a man walked out. As he passed under the dim light of the streetlamp, Arland was able to make out his features. *No mistake about it,* he thought to himself. *That's Dr. Laufer!*

Immediately, Arland bounded down from his lookout, two or three steps at a time. Racing across the open lawn, he called out, "Dr. Laufer! Dr. Laufer!" When he heard his name, Dr. Laufer stopped and looked up to see this figure running toward him in the dark. Arland slowed down to a fast walk as he neared Dr. Laufer, trying to catch his breath before speaking. Then he blurted out, "Dr. Laufer, I'm Arland Dwelle, the husband of Fran Dwelle."

"Oh, Mr. Dwelle. Yes, Mr. Dwelle. There you are. I'm glad I found you. I was looking for you in the waiting room."

With his heart in his throat, Arland asked, "How is my wife? How did the surgery go? Is she all right?"

"Oh yes, Mr. Dwelle, the operation went very well. Your wife is stable and in the recovery room now. She's doing fine."

"Oh, thank God!" Arland exclaimed. "Can you tell me, Doctor, what did her heart look like?"

"Well, her old heart was hard, stone-like, barely any movement, barely any heartbeat. She never could have lived much longer with that heart."

"And the new heart?" Arland asked.

"It's strong and healthy. I think she's going to be fine, Mr. Dwelle. Yes, she'll be just fine." And with a slight smile and a curt "goodnight," Dr. Laufer turned and walked away into the darkness.

Arland stood there for a few moments, inhaling deeply, exhaling slowly. He had no emotional energy left to respond to the news he had just received. No laughter. No shouts of joy. No tears of relief. The relentless heat of crisis after crisis after crisis had long ago dried up his well of emotions. But he still had one wellspring left—a heart of gratitude. Lifting his eyes to the sky, he whispered to heaven, "Thank you, Jesus. Thank you for sparing the wife I love. Thank you for giving my girls back their mother. Thank you for giving Fran a new heart. Thank you for this excellent medical team. Thank you, thank you, Lord. 'You have turned my wailing into dancing and clothed me with joy.'"

He went back into the hospital and gave our friends the good news—all had gone well, and I was doing fine! After rejoicing together, they joined hands in a circle and gave thanks in prayer. There in the hospital waiting room, in the wee hours of the morning, Pastor Danny led them in singing together The Doxology:

> *Praise God from whom all blessings flow /*
> *Praise Him all creatures here below /*
> *Praise Him above ye heavenly hosts /*
> *Praise Father, Son and Holy Ghost / Amen.*

Next, Arland called home, but our daughters were asleep. So, he told Nancy the good news. And when she relayed it to the girls in the morning, they began laughing and hugging and crying out, "Yes! Yes!" Then he called to the U.S. to give the wonderful report to my parents, his own mother, and Greg and Sandie. After one more attempt, he was able at last to reach Kaci, who was both shocked and thrilled to hear that I had just received a new heart.

Finally, he left the hospital building and went to his car. He sat behind the steering wheel and closed his eyes for a few moments. *Just for a minute or two*, he thought. He tried to absorb all that had transpired in the past ten hours. But far too much had happened in far too short a time. And he was far too weary to process it all.

Arland never made it home that night. Bobby Beard, who had driven through the night from Slovenia, found Arland in the morning, still sitting in the hospital parking lot, fast asleep in the driver's seat of his car.

Finally, . . . finally, . . . Arland could rest. My fight was over. And so was his.

Our battle had been won.

God's will had been done.

# Day Eighty-Seven

I slowly came to, gagging on my blood. Tubes everywhere were coming out of my mouth and stomach. I felt pressure on my side, dull pain in my chest, and heaviness from the tightly wrapped bandages. I thought, *I'm alive, I'm not in heaven, I made it through.* And then quickly it dawned on me—*I had the surgery! It actually happened!* My next thought was . . . *But God, You could have done it another way.* I wasn't saying it bitterly. I was just saying . . . *I know You could have . . . I thought You would have . . . But You didn't . . . Instead, You did it another way. Thank you, God, I'm alive!*

Right to the very end, I had expected God to heal my heart. But lying there in the recovery room, I realized I would never see that hope fulfilled in that way. For a few moments, I was in shock—*You didn't heal me, Lord!* My dream had been shattered. The specific healing I had prayed for and waited for was *never, ever* going to happen. Yet my hope and trust in God's character had *not* been shattered. As the reality of all that had happened sank in, I prayed, *God, even though I don't understand yet, I still trust You are good, wise, and loving, and I know You will help and strengthen me every day in my "new now."*

While lying there in semi-shock, I looked around the room, gradually taking in my surroundings. The huge window next to my bed was wide open. A warm June breeze was blowing into the room. I could hear birds chirping and street sounds from the cars in the parking lot below. *That's strange,* I thought, *aren't they concerned that a brand-new heart transplant patient is being exposed to all the dust and dirt from the street? Aren't I supposed to be extra careful about the risk of danger from germs?* After a few more minutes, I slipped off back to sleep.

A short time later, I woke up again, gagging and coughing up blood. I could see Arland standing outside my room talking to a very young man. After a few minutes, the man came into my room followed by Arland. He introduced himself saying, "Hello, Mrs. Dwelle, I'm Dr. Simon, the surgeon who did your heart transplant." I was surprised! He was so young—maybe late twenties. In flawless English, he told me everything had gone well, and he expected my recovery to go well, too. He also informed me that the donor heart came from a 22-year-old woman in Germany.

Arland greeted me with a big smile, kissed me on the cheek, and brought me a dozen red roses. He was beside himself with joy! "I'm so glad you're okay, Fran." We marveled together at the incredible sequence of events that had transpired in a short 24-hour period. Arland told me he had asked Dr. Laufer what my old heart looked like. (I was so glad he thought of doing that.) When I heard that Dr. Laufer said my old heart was like a stone, it helped me accept . . . at last! . . . that God's will was not to heal my damaged heart. Instead, the new heart I had received was God's way of healing me. It was *His healing in a surprise package!*

Later, Dr. Laufer described for me what actually happened the moment my new heart was transplanted. "When they sewed the new heart into your chest, it immediately pumped blood. In fact, it had such life that blood just gushed through it." He added, "Sometimes we have difficulty getting the new heart to start pumping, and we have to take extra measures. But your heart just burst with life." His initial assessment on the fateful phone call had been, "Mrs. Dwelle, this heart is perfect for you." And he was so right!

Arland also told me that during the surgery, my parents in California had been praying all day long. At one point my mother turned on a Christian radio station and heard the announcer reading the Scripture verse that says, "I will remove from you your heart of stone and give you a heart of flesh (Ezekiel 36:26)." That day also my father was reminded in prayer of a meaningful Bible verse: "And as you lay there in your blood, I said to you, 'Live!'" (Ezekiel 16:6) Both my parents felt the Lord had assured them that I was going to make it through the surgery. These wonderful reports helped me accept that the heart transplant was God's will for my life.

I was expected to be in ICU for 24 hours, but my recovery went so well they moved me out after 12 hours. I went back to the general ward where the three women patients had stared at me the night before. My coughing-up-blood had subsided, and my vital signs had improved. But I was still dealing with pain and breathing difficulties. In addition, I now heard an echo in my chest cavity after each heartbeat. It was unsettling, to say the least, and it was most noticeable when the room was quiet. I told Dr. Simon, "It seems like my heart echoes because it's too small for the hole in my chest." He said yes—that was precisely the case. Because my damaged heart had become enlarged, my chest cavity also became enlarged to accommodate it. He assured me that in a couple weeks the chest cavity would shrink back around the new heart, and the echo after each beat would stop. And it did.

Later, the solemn gravity of the whole experience hit me. I was alive because a young German woman had died. My new heart wasn't "free" at all. There was a tremendous cost—her life! She was a valuable person whom God loved and created. Who was she? What was her name? Where did she live? A family lost a beloved daughter. Her death inflicted on them a wound that will never heal. While my family was rejoicing, her family was experiencing great sorrow. She died (not by choice), and I now live. It is a sobering reality that will always be with me, and I will never take this gift for granted.

# Days Eighty-Eight to One Hundred

On the second day, Kaci, Jessi, and Cami came to visit me. They were elated to see how well I was doing. Each of them had experienced my illness in different ways. Kaci had missed most of the day-to-day trauma of my trips back and forth to the hospital. She had come home from college for a few weeks after my second heart attack, and then not again until the day after my transplant. As the oldest, she took charge when she was home, especially providing care for Cami. She visited me daily, and we chatted about college life, her friends, and her future plans. One day she shared with me a scripture verse that had encouraged her: "Heal me, O Lord, and I will be healed; save me and I will be saved for You are the one I praise." (Jeremiah 17:14). She tried to keep an upbeat tone when at home and an encouraging tone when with me: "You're going to make it through this, Mom." She felt my ordeal showed her the power of praying the Scriptures, and it gave her faith that God really does listen to prayer.

Jessica came to see me two or three times a week, but she dreaded the visits. She was sensitive as a child, and my affliction—combined with the sights, smells, and sounds in my hospital room—disturbed and unsettled her. She had always been a very affectionate daughter, hugging me often and freely, but she became subdued, sad, and withdrawn as my health had declined. Not knowing if I would live or die had left her reeling emotionally and spiritually—she didn't know what to believe anymore. She wrestled with honest questions about God, herself, faith, doubt, and guilt during that time. She didn't share her struggles with me, probably because she perceived I was too fragile to handle any more stress (which was undoubtedly true).

Cami was certainly aware of my health problems, but she didn't sink into despair. She believed everything was going to be okay, so she adapted more easily to the changes caused by my health issues. When she came after school to visit me, she would always climb on my bed so I could hold her. She did her homework in my hospital room, and then often we would play a game. She told her teacher that her mother had suffered a *herzinfarkt* (heart attack). But no one—teacher, classmates, or parents—gave her any emotional support or empathy. Thankfully, her church friends gave her the needed support.

As I listened to my three daughters that day, I could tell how relieved they were that our family nightmare seemed to be coming to an end. I was glad they had survived my ordeal *relatively* unscathed, but later I would wonder about the lasting effect the crisis left upon them. I had regrets that I wasn't more in tune with their daily struggles. I wish I had asked them more questions about how they were feeling and coping. I wish I had encouraged their faith more and boosted their hope. But my weak condition left me unable to help them as I would have liked. Thankfully, friends stepped in to regularly help and encourage them. None of the girls ever said that they felt neglected or alone. Maybe that was because, as someone told me, I did at least one parenting task right during this tumultuous time—I showed them how to trust God in times of hardship.

Ginger brought flowers the second day, and she and Danny came every day after that. During the entire ten-week crisis, from my second heart attack to the transplant, they had been there for us—mornings, afternoons, evenings, and all-night vigils. Their loving pastoral care for me and my family had gone way beyond the call of duty.

Dr. Melvin also visited me regularly, beginning with the second day. He was thrilled with my progress and with the excellent care I was receiving. I told him I was alarmed when I woke up from surgery next to a wide-open window with my incision fully exposed. I asked, "Is this standard medical procedure?"

He said this was not unusual because there are different philosophies regarding post-surgery isolation of the patient. "Vienna has a very relaxed policy," he said. "*Very* relaxed. They do not overly concern themselves about infection. Other transplant programs are very careful about exposure to infection. Stanford, for instance, has a more rigid policy in which transplant patients are isolated in a positive pressure environment. Other programs, like Pittsburg's, are more relaxed like Vienna's. On balance, both approaches appear to be all right, with neither one nor the other showing a great advantage in mortality rates." He concluded by reminding me, "You have nothing to worry about, Fran. Remember, the whole reason I'm in Vienna is because of their excellent program."

My recovery was remarkable in every way. In two days, I was walking up and down the hospital halls. After five days, I was climbing stairs. After seven days, the hospital did the first biopsy to see if my body was rejecting the heart. On a scale of 0 to 6, my heart had "0" rejection.

I was surprised how easily I adjusted to being in a six-bed ward. The women ranged in ages from 16 to 60. I chatted with them in English or simple German, and we quickly became acquainted. In spite of our cultural differences, we bonded over our mutual struggle of living with severe heart issues.

By the second week, I was totally pain-free and walking the hospital grounds four times a day. Plus, I had minimal side effects from the strict drug regimen I was on three times a day. And most amazingly of all, just fourteen days after the heart transplant, I was released from the hospital and sent home to a new life.

It had been exactly 100 days since my first heart attack. It also had been 100 days since I last walked in the Vienna Woods. So, on my first day home, my new heart and I had our first walk together in the Vienna Woods. With each grateful step, I fulfilled the promise from Scripture my daughter Cami had given me earlier in one of my darkest moments: *You will run and not be weary, you will walk and not faint.*

# The Next Year and Beyond

## Financial Provision

When the idea of a transplant was first proposed to us after my second heart attack, we were told it would be quite costly. At least $100,000. As foreigners, we were responsible for the full non-discounted charges. We thought our own medical insurance *might* cover the procedure, but we were not sure.

During a rare down time one day, I asked Arland, "Is this really worth it? All this cost to have a transplant?" It was all so overwhelming to me. I didn't actually say what I was thinking, *Would it be better if I just died so that you wouldn't have this huge bill?* Of course, despite my discouragement, I was fighting to live and didn't really want to die.

"Absolutely!" he replied. "Absolutely, it's worth it! Whatever it costs!" End of discussion from Arland!

So, we talked about selling our home in Wisconsin to come up with the money. We jokingly said, *a house for a heart;* in reality, though, it was not a joke. But in the weeks of my ordeal, we didn't have the energy—physically and mentally—to sell the house. When we learned we might have a six-month wait for a heart, we assumed we had ample time to sell our home.

But the transplant happened so quickly that we had no time to sell the house. In fact, we didn't have time to do *anything* about money. In the frantic rush to get to the hospital that day, Arland even forgot his checkbook. So, he didn't have the necessary deposit money required to admit a foreigner for surgery. The next day, Greg and Bobby came up with the required "advance" money (after the fact) to give to the hospital.

With our meager resources, the cost of paying for the transplant was an overwhelming challenge. I wondered how we could possibly pay such a huge bill. "Fran, we're just going to have to trust God again," Arland said. "He's brought us through so much in this entire crisis, so He's not going to abandon us now." We prayed together, asking God for a financial miracle.

The Vienna doctors knew the finances were a challenge for us. When they learned our American insurance would not cover the cost, they became our advocates with the hospital administration, often going out on a limb on our behalf. They were able to get my transplant cost approved for the same amount that an Austrian health insurance company would have to pay—*only* $50,000, but that was still an impossible mountain for us to climb. (An Austrian woman in my ward paid out-of-pocket 80 shillings total—less than $10—for her transplant!)

Unknown to us, our closest colleagues called our missions headquarters in Springfield, Missouri, and told the leaders about our situation. In one day, they raised over $30,000 through the sacrificial giving of missionaries and pastors gathered there for meetings from all over the world. Other individuals and churches from all over the U.S.—mostly people we did not know—also sent gifts. Within one month, the entire amount of $50,000 had been provided. Arland and I were overwhelmed by this outpouring of kindness. The Vienna doctors and staff also marveled at the generosity of so many on our behalf.

## Follow-up Treatment

During the first year, eight biopsies of my heart were done to determine whether my body was rejecting the new organ. All the biopsies showed zero rejection. Dr. Laufer happened to be the one doing the biopsies one day when I came in. He had not seen me for months, and he was surprised at how I looked. "I didn't even recognize you when you first came in," he said. "I was thinking of you as you were when you were so sick before your transplant. But you look nothing now like you did then. You're so . . . be – yu - ti – ful!" He laughed and I had to laugh, too.

One year later, I went to Stanford Medical Center for a comprehensive follow-up treatment. I checked in with Dr. Cooley, the head hematologist at Stanford. I brought all my records from Vienna, handed them to him and said, "Here's what the doctors in Vienna think is wrong with my blood. What do you think?"

He leafed briefly through the papers and then threw them down on the table. With a chuckle he said, "I guess we at Stanford are kind of arrogant. We think if something hasn't been discovered at Stanford, or if we don't know about it, then we really don't put much stock in it. I've never heard of this study, so we'll just do our own testing first and see what we come up with."

"Of course, that will be fine," I said. For the next two weeks, I went through innumerable tests from many doctors, leaving me black and blue all over. Every few days, they would bring me into a conference room and go over the test results: *negative, negative, negative.* Naturally, I was delighted to hear all the *negatives,* but I wondered if they would find some other cause for my heart troubles.

After two weeks, Dr. Cooley said, "Well, Mrs. Dwelle, I think it's possible these Vienna doctors are on to something after all." He contacted Dr. Sinzinger and asked him to send all the medical data they had on me. After comparing Vienna's results with their own studies, he said, "I think the doctors in Vienna are correct. You do have a defect in the platelets of your blood that causes clots to form spontaneously. It's very rare, something we've never heard of before." And he prescribed the same treatment as Vienna did—one baby aspirin a day.

For many years, I returned to Stanford annually for my checkups. And each time the test results were the same: one wonderful *negative* after another. Their lead transplant surgeon said to me on one of my visits, "You are a living miracle! Your overall health is amazing! You don't even look like a heart transplant recipient. If it wasn't for your scar, I would never guess that you are one."

## Dr. David Melvin

A week after my transplant, Dr. Melvin's year of sabbatical study ended, and he moved back to Cincinnati, Ohio. He truly had been my angel in white (as I had told him on the day of my surgery). Beginning with the second devastating heart attack, he had visited me almost every day I was in the hospital. With his upbeat personality, he always brought me encouragement. He was there supporting Arland during the transplant, and with me every day after the transplant.

Looking back on his year in Vienna, he felt his greatest purpose in being there was to prepare me to deal with the challenges I would face the rest of my life. He saw it as divine providence that he was in that place at that time. Originally, he had come to Vienna to perfect the development of a mechanical heart, but my ordeal had shown him that a heart transplant is a much better solution than a mechanical heart. "Seeing how much difference an organ graft can make in the life of an individual and a family," he said, "has inspired me to go back into heart transplant surgery."

When I saw him again one year later, we had a joyful reunion. He couldn't help but marvel—almost in disbelief—at how well I looked. From the very beginning, he had said that a heart transplant would improve my life immeasurably, and I was living proof of how right he had been.

## Greg and Sandie Mundis

The day after my transplant, Greg and Sandie called me from the States. Naturally, they were elated to hear the surgery had gone well. They both had felt so strongly that a heart transplant was the only answer for my health. And I was very mindful of the fact that Greg had urged me to take *this* heart, not to wait for another one. When they returned to Vienna two months later, Arland and I picked them up at the airport. Seeing us at *Arrivals*, they ran out and hugged us and then hugged us some more. Greg was weeping, Sandie was laughing and crying. They could not believe how well I looked. Sandie kept saying, "Look at her! Her color is back! Look at her new haircut! Just look at her!" They came to our home for a big meal I had prepared, something I could have never done before. They kept saying that evening, "I can't believe this is the same person. You're like the old Fran!" Throughout that night, they celebrated what God had done for me.

## One-Year Anniversary

On June 17, the one-year anniversary of my heart transplant, we went to the AKH hospital. We walked through the same doors where I had walked out with a new heart. We went to the top of the flight of steps where Arland had watched the operation in the middle of the night. That stairway was like a sacred place to us, an altar of thanks to remind us of God's goodness. Then we drove up to the famous *Schloss Wilhelminenberg*. There we looked down on the hospital rooms where I had often looked out the window and prayed, "Lord, help me walk again on those palace grounds." At that memorial place, with a panoramic view of the hospital, we gave thanks for my renewed health and all the medical personnel, doctors, and nurses in Vienna who had worked tirelessly to save my life.

## Setbacks

In the year following the transplant, I began to wonder how I could live well. I was taking anti-rejection drugs, so I knew being immuno-suppressed made me susceptible to many kinds of physical ailments. I started to become fearful. But God calmed me through his Word. One Sunday when our pastor quoted John 10:10, "I have come that they may have life and have it to the full." I instantly knew God was saying that I was not to worry any longer. He was going to strengthen me to live life to the fullest.

The first setback came three months after the transplant. I contracted an infection in the hospital. For many days it was low-grade, but then it got into my bloodstream and went throughout my whole body. I was put on a drug therapy, but it did not help. A few days later, in the middle of the night, I awoke with a temperature of almost 105°. Arland frantically rushed me to the hospital where they hooked me up to a strong intravenous solution of antibiotics. By this time, I had become delirious, and I started to fear I was going to die. But God calmed my fears and reduced my fever to normal in just four hours. Eventually, the doctors isolated the infection as *e coli* bacteria. I was hospitalized for five days, and my life was spared.

The second incident occurred ten years after my transplant. We were living in Bismarck, North Dakota, and my life was going along beautifully. I was active and strong, with zero rejection after many years of biopsies. Then, one day I felt weak and sick with a high fever, so I assumed I had the flu. Arland urged me to see my cardiologist. I thought it was a waste of time, but I did it anyway. I had an EKG and blood work done, feeling fairly certain nothing critical was wrong. All of a sudden, my doctor—looking grim—came back with the results. "I believe your heart is in rejection," he blurted out. "You need to see your transplant doctor right away!" I was stunned and started to cry.

Immediately, we flew to Stanford Hospital the next day to see my transplant doctor. She wasted no time running a battery of tests on me. It was confirmed—my heart was in a late stage of rejection. We were all shocked! She said they would try to do everything possible to reverse the rejection, but she gave no assurance of the outcome. Thankfully, God was gracious again. The heart rejection was reversed, and there was minimal damage to my heart. The whole ordeal lasted three weeks. When it was over, I was happy I had followed Arland's suggestion to see the doctor immediately, in spite of my doubts!

## Percentages

On the night I was so distraught about signing for a heart transplant, Arland had prayed, "Lord, help Fran beat all the percentages." When I had my transplant in 1992, Vienna's one-year survival rate was 90%, and their five-year survival rate was 80%. Both percentages were among the best in the world. The benchmark for survival was the five-year anniversary of the transplant because that was when significant mortality began to happen. But with the advent of the anti-rejection drug cyclosporine, the old stats became skewed as transplant recipients started living longer. In 1992, the longest anyone had lived with a cardiac transplant was 21 years. But by 2021, the longevity record for living with a transplanted heart had increased to 36 years. Dr. Zuckerman, the transplant coordinator for my surgery, speculated that one day heart recipients might live 40 or even 50 years if they have no other problems. We haven't seen that yet but, by God's grace, I'm now at 29 years and counting! When I had my transplant, I was hoping to live long enough—9 years—to see my youngest daughter graduate from high school. But now I've had the joy of seeing all three daughters finish high school and college, launch careers, get married, and bless us with five granddaughters. I'm thankful every day to be living a good and full life.

# Epiphany

During the weeks after the transplant, I told many people my story—at least, *most* of the story. But I did not tell anyone the *whole* story. I kept one part hidden away—the nighttime encounter with The Visitor in my hospital room. Only Arland knew about it. Then one day, while sharing my medical journey with my brother Joe, who is a pastor in America, I decided to tell him about Jesus' appearance to me. He was quite amazed and said, "Fran, why haven't you told anyone about this? We knew the basic story of how you got a new heart, but why have none of us heard about your vision of the Lord? This is the most incredible part of the story!"

"First of all," I said, "it was not a vision; it was a *visit*. Jesus walked into my room—He was there *in person*. I felt His power flow into my body. I knew without a doubt He had come to heal me. And I *was* better. The doctors all noticed it the next day. But still, my heart was not healed. So, I kept waiting for Him to complete the healing of my heart. But as you know, that never happened. So, I guess I've never told anyone about that night because I don't really know why Jesus visited me. After all this time, it still remains a mystery to me. If it wasn't to heal me, then why?"

My brother said, "Fran, what were all of us asking God to do for you? Heal your damaged heart, right? Family, friends, and churches were all praying the same thing: *Lord, please heal Fran's heart*. We all

153

thought that a healing was what you needed more than anything else in life."

"Yes, obviously, that's how people were praying for me."

"But the Lord knew there was one thing He could give you that was *better* than a healed heart. It was—"

"It was Jesus!" I interjected. "Yes, of course! I see it now! It was Jesus I needed more than anything else! It was His presence I needed more than anything else! That's what He came to tell me that night: *I am a better gift to you than a healing!* That's what He was trying to say to me! *My presence is all you need in life!* Yes, now it's all clear to me! That explains why I never had any fear. Because I always knew—through His Word and through prayer—He was *present* with me. I was never alone and never without hope. That's why I clung daily to all those Scriptures, the ones that reminded me He *is* my present help, He *is* my strength, He *is*, He *is*, He *is*! It all makes sense now."

My brother responded, "Yes, Fran, you got to experience physically what the rest of us only know by faith—that *the presence of Jesus is everything we need.* Perhaps that's now the message of your life."

And I concur; finally, it all makes sense to me. My life message comes out of my life experience that God Himself is the best gift in life we could ever hope to have.

After the transplant, my friend Elizabeth Mittelstaedt said to me, "Fran, now God has given you a story to be told." She had mentioned to me a year earlier, "It's stories that communicate to women." My thought at that time was, *I don't even have a story to tell, at least nothing like Joni Eareckson Tada's or Corrie Ten Boom's.* So, I had prayed, *God, give me a story to tell . . . but don't make it something that's too difficult to live through.* I thought perhaps He would show me how to put the life experiences I had already been through into a "story." I never imagined it would be something as unusual and dramatic as a heart transplant!

Two years after my heart transplant, a shortened version of my story was featured in the German magazine, *"Lydia,"* the largest

Christian women's magazine in Europe.[1] A photo of my daughter Cambria was on the cover with the caption, *"Even Mommy's New Heart Beats for Me."* This magazine issue was the first one ever to go into East Germany. The Berlin wall had recently been torn down with the defeat of Communism. The East German women were spiritually open and hungry after decades of repressed religion. Elizabeth Mittelstaedt, the editor, believed my story would give hope to women and wrote, "When troubles come, do we wonder where God is? By taking a look at Fran's life, it is easy to discover how close God was during this time, just as He promises in His Word."

One year later my story was published in *"Radost," (Joy)* Magazine, a Croatian Christian women's magazine.[2] This was the first issue to be printed after the Yugoslavian war when women had suffered great distress and sadness. I marveled at the unique timing. Both magazines published the story right after years of hardship and oppression in East Germany and Yugoslavia. I was amazed and thankful to see how God used my story in ways I never imagined.

Shortly after the transplant, I talked to my friend Myrna who had asked me earlier to tell her what I found when I reached the bottom of the pit. I told her, "Yes, I think I did make it to the bottom of the pit, or at least very close to the bottom. And what I found there was no surprise—I found the Lord! I found His love there, just as I have found it at every other place in my life."

Arland said to me one day, "Fran, do you realize that your life is a living metaphor of what the gospel is?"

"In what way," I asked?

"Someone died so that you could live," he replied. "You have a new heart only because of the death of another person. In the same way, Christ died to replace our spiritually damaged hearts and give us new life."

So, this truth is part of my life message, too. My physical experience *does* have a spiritual parallel. When my physical heart—

---

1   Mittelstaedt, Elizabeth. (1993, Second Quarter). *Nur einen Herzschlag vom Tod entfernt [Only a heartbeat away from death]. Lydia Magazine, 4-7.*

2   Mittelstaedt, Elizabeth. (1994, Third Quarter). *Samo Jedan Otkucaj Srca Do Smrti* [Only a heartbeat away from death]. *Radost Magazine, 4-7.*

the center of my body—didn't function well, then my whole body wouldn't work. Similarly, if my spiritual heart—the center of my spiritual being—doesn't function right, my spiritual health also suffers. As the Proverb says, "Above all else, guard your heart, for it is the wellspring of life."

I asked Arland one day if he remembers my ever mentioning that I might die if I refused the donor heart and then wasn't healed. He said, "I don't remember us talking about this, but I'm pretty sure we both thought about it." He added, "So then you'd get to heaven and ask God, 'Why didn't you heal me?' And God would say, 'What are you talking about? I sent you a heart and you refused it!'"

So, it's true—I *do* have a story to tell about God healing me. But it's not the life message I would have chosen. If it had been up to me, I would have chosen a different story—one where God instantly healed my damaged heart. But God chose another way of healing—a transplanted heart. He chose the story that would be for my good and for His glory.

And I am eternally grateful.

# Coda

For our 25th wedding anniversary, Arland and I drove to the *Carinthia* region of Austria to see the *Hochosterwitz* Castle. This medieval fortress and stronghold was built around A.D. 1200 on a mountainous cone rising 564 feet above the valley floor. We walked up a 2000-foot winding path that curved around the mountain to the top. Along the way, we passed through 14 fortified gates and crossed over five drawbridges. This castle had never been conquered, though it had been attacked and besieged numerous times. Legend has it that no enemies ever even got past the fourth gate. At the top of this impregnable fortress, we reached a square tower built into the mountainous rock. This tower, the "castle keep," was the place where residents of the castle and village locals would flee to escape their attackers. In the face of impending death, it was their sure place of safety.[3]

As we stood at the top looking out over the valley below, Arland said, "Look where we're at, Fran. Can you believe what you just did? You walked all the way up this mountain less than one year after having a heart transplant!"

"Yes, I agree that is quite amazing. But I think there's one thing even more amazing. Look where I've ended up. Not just at the top of this mountain. But to the *tower* at the top of this mountain."

---

3  Hochosterwitz Castle. (2020, October 23). Retrieved from http://www.en.wikipedia.org/wiki/Hochosterwitz_Castle

I was awestruck as I realized the symbolic significance of this place. For I knew *what* the tower represented in Scripture. Or more accurately, *who* the tower represented. I had meditated on this countless times in my darkest hours and sleepless nights. The tower was the Lord; He was my strong place. The tower was the Lord; He was my safe place. In times of trouble, times of trial, and times of trauma, I had been running into the Tower again and again my whole life.

As a young girl, drowning in deep deadly waters, I ran to Him. And I was safe.

As a missionary, struggling in a foreign culture, I ran to Him. And I was safe.

As a mother, hearing her daughters say goodbye, I ran to Him. And I was safe.

As a woman, needing healing for her heart, I ran to Him. And I was safe.

As a transplant recipient, facing a myriad of risks, I ran to Him. And I was safe.

So, on June 1, 1993, our 25th anniversary, Arland and I stood by the castle tower, high above the valley, and we gave thanks for how God had spared me from certain death. We also committed the future of my health to His care. For should danger ever befall me again, I will do once more what I have done my whole life . . .

I will run to the Lord . . .

And . . .

I will be safe.

*The name of the Lord is a strong tower.*
*The righteous run into it,*
*And they are safe.*
Proverbs 18:10

# Afterword

### The Phone Call
### (Reimagined)

"Mrs. Dwelle,
We have a heart for you!"
You do? Who is this we?
It's us—your doctors, nurses, and medical staff.
We've prepared ourselves for years so
You could once again be healthy.
Oh, thank you, Austrians,
For my new heart!

"Mrs. Dwelle,
We have a heart for you!"
You do? Who is this we?
It's us—your friends, your brothers and sisters.
We've prayed hours, days and weeks so
You could have this gift of healing.
Oh, thank you, friends,
For my new heart!

"Mrs. Dwelle,
We have a heart for you!"
You do? Who is this we?
It's us—your husband and your daughters.
We've begged the Lord for mercy so
You'd still be our wife and mother.
Oh, thank you, dear family,
For my new heart!

"Mrs. Dwelle,
We have a heart for you!"
You do? Who is this we?
It's Me.
Oh, thank you, God!
I'm glad you finally called!

# Acknowledgements

There are three main contributing sources for the details in this true story:

1) Many hours of taped conversations in Vienna between Joe, my brother and co-author, Arland, and me a few months after the transplant. Our fresh and clear memories of all details during that time period were vital as we wrote the story.

2) A taped interview with Dr. Andreas Zuckerman, Heart Transplant Coordinator at the *AKH* in Vienna, on February 22, 1996. The content in Day Eighty-Six (3) is from this interview.

3) Arland's and my personal journal entries written during those days.

# THANKS and APPRECIATION

1. To my husband Arland--for his constant love, encouragement, and wise counsel.

2. To my brother and co-author Joe Ferrante--for his vision to tell my story, and his time, talent, and perseverance to make it happen.

3. To my daughters Kaci, Jessica, Cambria and to my sister Norene Antin--for their emotional support and kindness; to my granddaughter Gianna--for her computer help.

4. To my prayer-triplet partners Marcia Fahn and Diane Benes and to many other friends--for their faithful prayers and encouragement.

5. To the excellent doctors and medical personnel at the *Wilhelminenspital* in Vienna and at the heart transplant centers of the *AKH/Allgemeines Krankenhaus* (Vienna General Hospital), Stanford University Hospital in CA, and Abbott NW Hospital in Minneapolis, MN—for being the instruments in God's gracious hand for my care.

6. And most of all, to Jesus Christ. *"For to me, to live is Christ, and to die is gain."* (Philippians 1:21)

**Thanks and Appreciation from Joe:** To my wife Mary Jo who tenaciously cheered on the writer-in-me until the book crossed the finish line.

# Closing Words

Dear Reader,

Thank you for reading my story. I trust you found hope and encouragement through it.

My heart-transplant journey has been for me a dramatic metaphor with a profound spiritual message. I recognized that this experience was reminiscent of what happened to me when I became a follower of Jesus Christ. Yes, a physical heart transplant is a wonderful thing. But a new life—an eternal life—given to one by God is truly a miracle!

I have written a post entitled *Ten Heart Transplant Analogies* which you can find on my website, www.frandwelle.com.

With thanks and appreciation,

**Fran Dwelle**
www.frandwelle.com
www.joemferrante.com

Would you please give an online book review?
Thank you!

# Photos

Fran and family joyfully leaving the Vienna hospital two weeks after her heart transplant.

Dwelle family in Vienna nine months after Fran's heart transplant.

*Fran and her brother and co-author Joe Ferrante one year after her heart transplant.*

Die christliche Zeitschrift
für die Frau

D 12013 F
2/93

2. Quartal 1993
DM 4,25 · sfr. 4,25
öS 35,—

# Lydia

Mutter im Beruf

Die Tränen der Frauen
auf dem Balkan

„Ben Hur"
und eine betende Frau

Neid, Neid, Neid

Wie sehe ich bloß aus?

Wenn das Stillen nicht klappt

Aids-Tragödie

AUCH MUTTIS
NEUES
HERZ SCHLÄGT
FÜR
MICH

Daughter Cambria on cover of German magazine, "Lydia," with
title caption
*Even Mommy's New Heart Beats for Me.*

Fran and Arland on their 50<sup>th</sup> wedding anniversary in 2018.

# Author Profiles

**Fran Dwelle** has been engaged in Christian service for many years in Europe and the U.S. as a teacher, mentor, and leader. She was active in the early gatherings of "Hope for Europe—Women in Leadership." She is the founder and president of JOY, an interdenominational women's ministry, and the creator of www.pray3.org, which equips women in *triplet prayer*. She enjoys playing the piano, cooking Italian, and reading. She has three married daughters and five granddaughters which are her pride and joy. She enjoys life with her husband Arland in Bismarck, North Dakota.

**www.frandwelle.com**

**Joe Ferrante** (MDiv) pastored for 25 years and now travels teaching on *The Extravagant Love of God*. He enjoys playing the piano, eating Italian, and reading. He and his wife Mary Jo live in Santa Rosa, California, and have three children, four grandchildren, and two great-grands.

**www.joemferrante.com**

Manufactured by Amazon.ca
Bolton, ON

27253343R00101